Celia Hart

It's never too late to love or rebel

Selected writings edited by Walter Lippmann

Socialist Resistance, London

Published by Socialist Resistance, July 2006.
Second printing, August 2006.

Articles copyright © CubaNews, 2003-2006.
Cover photograph © Michael Hopwood, 2003.
Printed in Britain by Lightning Source.

ISBN 978-0-902869-99-8

Socialist Resistance would be glad to have readers' opinion of this book, its translations and design, and any suggestions you may have for future publications.

Socialist Resistance books are available at special quantity discounts to educational and non-profit organizations, and to booksellers.

To contact us, please write to Socialist Resistance, PO Box 1109, London N4 2UU, Britain or email contact@socialistresistance.net.

Contents

Publisher's acknowledgements

The articles in the book have been edited and selected by Walter Lippmann and appear with his kind permission. Most are translations by Joseph Mutti, Maria Montelibre and Ana Portela. Unsigned endnotes are courtesy of CubaNews. We have made minor corrections.

Walter Lippmann and other contributors to CubaNews bring to the attention of people concerned with Cuba a wide range of news and information about the island, the Cuban community abroad, Cuba's international relations, and related topics. Their email list provides powerful resources that assist activists in learning about Cuba, its politics and society. Readers can visit CubaNews online, and subscribe to it, at http://groups.yahoo.com/group/CubaNews. The primary language of that list is English; though some Spanish material is sent from time to time. CubaNews has played an invaluable role in allowing English-reading activists the opportunity to access a wealth of information. This book is part of that wealth.

The opening article in this book, "Fidel and Trotsky" is an interview with Celia Hart which first appeared in Rouge, the weekly newspaper of the French section of the Fourth International; the Revolutionary Communist League (LCR). Its English translation, and the article '"Welcome"... Trotsky', appear with the permission of the Fourth International's English-language review, internationalviewpoint.org. "Ivan couldn't defeat Fidel" is an edited and partially retranslated version of a CubaNews article published by laborstandard.org: our warmest thanks go to them also.

Finally, our heartfelt gratitude goes to Michael Hopwood for his kind permission to use his photograph of a Cuban flag, which is used on the cover of this volume.

August, 2006.

Fidel and Trotsky

Q: For fifteen years now the definitive collapse of Cuban society has been announced at regular intervals. Fidel Castro himself has stressed the development of inequality in Cuba. Can we preserve and develop these conquests or are they condemned to disappear?
A: I identify totally with the Cuban revolution but I don't represent it. What I say is my personal opinion. The social conquests of the socialist revolution in Cuba are obvious: great social equality, a system of education which is accessible to everyone and on a level comparable to the United States or Europe - in other words to much richer countries - a health system superior to any other country in Latin America and which, contrary to what is happening in Europe, is not being privatized or dismantled.

But if the Cuban revolution has been able to overcome the difficulties of the "special period" [1] - power cuts, breakdowns of public transport, minimal rations of food, etc. - the result of Cuban trade agreements with the countries of the so-called "socialist camp" and of the continuing imperialist blockade - it is because the Cuban population as a whole defended the revolution and not social advantages.

The difficulties that we are now experiencing are not related to material needs. The liberalization of trade and of possession of foreign currency - capitalist mechanisms that were introduced, and that some people justify by comparing them to the Russian NEP of the 1920s - led to social differentiation and the appearance of "the new rich".

In a speech on November 17 last year the commander [Fidel Castro] formulated it in the following way: "this revolution can destroy itself all alone, and the only ones who can't manage to destroy it are them" [the US, imperialism]. "But we can destroy it and it would be our fault". And he said that while stressing that: "several tens of thousands of parasites produce nothing and earn everything..."

Similarly, the Minister of Foreign Affairs, Felipe Perez Roque, insisted at the United Nations that the danger for Cuba was the creation of a bourgeois class. The interpenetration of the bureaucracy and the market economy, that's where the danger lies. We have to demolish the foundations of the bureaucracy, because it is on these foundations that the bourgeois class can develop - we saw in the USSR, in Poland, and elsewhere how the bureaucrats, who were managers, men of power, became owners, became capitalists.

In Cuba, unlike in the GDR of the 1980s, "Lenin is alive": the bureaucratic counterrevolution has not been carried through. We must take advantage of that to demolish the remaining foundations of the bureaucracy, because it is from there that the danger of capitalist restoration can come.

Q: The Venezuelan revolutionary process is making it possible to loosen the imperialist stranglehold around Cuba. And even if this process is only beginning and the parallels between the two revolutions are deceptive, can we speak today of reciprocal influences?

A: Cuban doctors, paramedics, and teachers, are working in Venezuela. But they don't take any part in the political life of the country, a choice with which I disagree, even though you can understand that there is a self-limitation to avoid Cuba being accused of interfering.

But the freshness of the Venezuelan process, the voyages there, the possibility of experiencing other realities and intervening there are an enriching experience and it is important that Cubans, in particular young people - and not the Cuban government or state of course - can take part in the Venezuelan revolution, not only as doctors or teachers, but in the factories, the neighborhood meetings etc.

In any case it has to be stressed that the links that have been established between Cuba and Venezuela are different from those that existed with the USSR. Because it is a question of links between two revolutionary processes, one which is already consolidated and another which is beginning. Both of them are authentic revolutions. With the USSR, on the contrary, it was a question of relations between states, and of unequal relations.

The dynamic of the Venezuela-Cuba tandem, the possible integration of Bolivia into the process that is under way, actualizes the permanent revolution and enables us to lay the foundations of a relationship that is going in the direction of building a real united front.

Q: Why does Trotsky's theoretical contribution seems so important to you?

A: In Cuba we have been living through a process of permanent revolution since the Moncada [2].

The continuity of the revolution, the question of its deepening, was at the centre of the thinking of Cuban revolutionaries, and especially of the July 26 Movement. First of all Mella [3], then Guevara, were accused of being "Trotskyists". They weren't, but the accusations had a rational kernel, because they were oriented towards the permanent revolution even without having read Trotsky. The permanence of the Cuban revolution is in the ideas of the Left Opposition.

In Cuba anti-Stalinist feeling has always existed, because people thought that communism was the Stalinism of the Communist Party. And the Communist Party was one of the last to join the revolution...But when Fidel announced in 1961 the socialist character of the Cuban revolution, people said: "If Fidel is a communist, you can sign me up too".

I always felt that there was something missing in my thinking about the revolution. That's what I've found through reading Trotsky: I discovered that social justice and individual freedom were not contradictory and that we weren't condemned to choose between them, that socialism could only be built by walking on both feet.

Published in Rouge, May, 2006.

NOTES

[1] The "special period" is the term used to describe the difficult situation that Cuba found itself in after the collapse of the Soviet Union, from which it is only now emerging

[2] On July 26, 1953, Fidel Castro was arrested after the failure of the attack against the Moncada barracks. Defending himself in court, he made a speech which has gone down in history under the name of "History will absolve me", in which he outlined the perspective of a revolutionary struggle against the Batista dictatorship

[3] Julio Antonio Mella (1903-1929) was a founder of the Cuban Communist party and is considered a hero by the present Cuban Government. At the time of his death, he was in exile in Mexico. In Mexico he wrote for a number of newspapers, including Tren Blindado ("The armored Train" a Trotsky symbol). He embarrassed the pro-Moscow leadership of the Cuban Communist party by trying to organize the overthrow of the Cuban government of General Gerardo Machado. In 1928, Mella was expelled from the Mexican Communist party for associating with Trotskyists. Diego Rivera and others have speculated that Mella was killed by Vittorio Vidali, an Italian Stalinist involved in the murder of over 400 radicals, including Leon Trotsky [Publisher's note].

It's never too late to love or rebel...

No need for concern. I'm not saying there's a wave of revolution crossing Europe. I only mean that it's never too late to start, and if the hum begins with beautiful France, it is not utopian to dream...

It's not as if the young people of African and Arab descent are seeking to retake the Bastille, although in passing it's likely that Nicolás Sarkozy would end up on the guillotine for being such a stupid, racist fascist all in one. Many "well-born" French are only ever grateful for a racial mix on the soccer field, and support the Nazi Minister of the Interior who has promised them he will clean the streets of France of those "thieves and scum".

Neither is it as if these young people intend to form another Commune, or even that they will be able to give us another May '68 in winter. I only mean that the sound of burning cars is far more than an ethnic disturbance, because a little more than a month ago French workers carried out a wonderful strike that ground the city to a halt. Something is wrong with the government. What? It turns out that even in cultured France, capitalism also smells badly and that the "South" is to be found there, as in every country. Perhaps this is the recourse of today's capitalism: to sow the "South" within its own territories. We might be on the point of reaching the saturation point of a system that is not able to solve its own contradictions, and that in turn the switched-off Left will not be able to react. The result, of course, is that history will not wait until we've finished reading our old notebooks.

Beautiful things have been written describing what began as an incident in the Parisian suburb of Clichy-sous-Bois, ending in the tragic death of two French youths of immigrant African families. The episode has become one of national importance forcing the government to institute curfews for several months. The wave of fires that embraced all of France demonstrates to us that nothing under the sun is new, and that what takes place in the French suburbs is the same (in its way) as that which took place in the streets of Buenos Aires at the end of 2001.

Perhaps today Europe is less prepared to assimilate these rumblings, but history is being shaken once again - a modern reflection of social dissent which is the first phase of class struggle. It contains the same social nuances which astounded us when Hurricane Katrina flung itself upon our fellow beings in the Mississippi Basin. Immigration problems present the serious social conflicts of the world in yet another way.

The teenagers electrocuted in Clichy-sous-Bois are martyrs in this class struggle. Yes! Of course, many will accuse me of idealistic "pamphletism", but to be some kind of protagonist in this voiceless fight that has gestated in Europe's belly doesn't necessarily mean shouting out segments of the Communist Manifesto or identifying with the Left. The vicissitudes of the 20th century that many think have ended demonstrate to us that to say, to be, and to do are verbs that are abysmally distanced in politics.

A recent article in La Brèche by Orlando Núñez Grove points out:

"Migrants have become one of those subjects of injustice and resistance, as much for the most productive segments of the new world proletariat in the big metropolitan capitals, as for the relatives of migrants from the hamlets located on the outskirts that await their monthly family remittances."

This is not the first time that migrants have risen up in the cities, exploding with fury.

For more than a century, the workers of the world have celebrated May Day as International Workers Day. But with time our memories lapse. After those pathetic Moscow May Day marches which were so perfectly and precisely organized with their tanks, their infantry, their splendid artillery and their sad conceit of power - identical to the Berlin marches in the 1930s - the true character of the 1886 Chicago demonstrations has faded. There is not the least nostalgia for those marches with tanks and airplanes, but these French youths - and French they are – remind us with their burning cars of those days of the Chicago anarchists who mobilized European migrant workers in the United States.

José Martí wrote a chronicle of those days, and his first sympathies for those socialist ideas summoning us now can be found in these writings:

"The United States, which is made up of immigrants, is already actively seeking a way to limit excessive or pernicious immigration: watching from where evil enters the United States, it can get rid of those countries that have not been over-run by its generosity - at the risk of injecting poisoned blood into their veins - or its limitless desire to expand."

But Martí died exactly when imperialism began to explicitly take hold of the world. No imperialist power – including France - "could get rid of their limitless longing to expand." And today to sow the "South" in the North might be the only way out that those countries have, in their need for an underemployed work force. Migration towards rich countries sustains many underdeveloped countries through remittances sent home.

We have in migration then, whether the books say it or not, a potent subject of the current history of the world, because migrants are not only the waste of consumer societies, they are also responsible for the economic survival of many poor countries.

To avoid too much satisfaction, I try not to imagine forces of organized migrant workers conscious of their historical role within the societies of imperialist powers.

I read somewhere that the methods of these French youths are not considered to be legitimate by the labor movement - that sabotaging cars, day-care centers, etc. are unworthy of the proletariat.

Who has the right to speak of correct methods and civic attitudes to those who live at the bottom of the world's barrel?

The La Brèche article argues forcefully that "the Third World has come to the First World. The cities need slaves, but cannot assimilate them as citizens. They are not unionized because they don't have proper employment; they are not trades people because they have no heritage; they are not legally organized because they don't have permission. They are simple insurrectionists, marginalized, testifying to the contradictions of globalization."

That is how it is. In a way, the Bible is right, when it says that the last will be the first. It is rhetorical and absurd to force the Earth to rotate in the other direction. Better for those of us on the supposed "Left" to hurry and see with whom we will definitively throw in our luck.

"What do they want?" Martí wonders in his chronicle of labor immigrants from 19th century Chicago. He responds: "A day's wage, another day of respect ... they want working hours to be no more than eight, not so much for some light to enter their souls as they rest, but so that the manufacturers are forced to employ those other workers that today don't have a job."

"What do they want?" wonders Orlando Núñez Grove of the immigrants in France a century and half later. The answer is that right now "they don't know what they want. Racism, humiliation and scorn, not to continue living the life they have had up to now, with heads held low, awaiting compassion, sensibility, understanding, solidarity, employment, health, education. In short, their rights."

They are full of hate. And who says that the hate is not legitimate to face the world? This world is contaminated with hate, and if those teenagers are full of it, it is because hate spouts like waste water in the sewers of the French suburbs.

This doesn't come from me. Ernesto Che Guevara said that "a people without hate cannot triumph over a brutal enemy." And Sarkozy and company are brutal enemies.

For that reason we of the Left need to avoid getting bogged-down and avoid looking from our organizational heights upon those who we don't consider to be the proletariat because they are underemployed or the wretched of the world. If they are not organized, if they cannot pull together with more cohesion, the blame doesn't only belong to them, but to us as "the organizers" who are not able to understand the direction the world is taking.

Our resplendent May Day that takes place every year replete with red flags was once pregnant with sabotage, bombs and fury.

The self-same José Martí, who as a first step in the struggle for justice rejected violence, ended by declaring in 1893 that: "It is legitimate and honorable to despise violence and to preach against it while there is viable and rational way to nonviolently obtain the justice indispensable to humankind's well-being. However, when it is obvious that - for deeply unavoidable, irreconcilable and different interests relating to diversity, political mindset and aspirations - a peaceful path will not obtain the least minimum rights of the people; when the people, experiencing a new fullness of being, find their abilities suffocated, or when peaceful efforts in the face of glaring truth are ignored and it becomes disloyal to the people not to react; I am determined to proclaim my support [for such methods]."

We would have to question if - faced with racism, alienation and the abandonment to which they are subjected by everyone - the nightmare in which poverty-stricken migrants live throughout Europe leaves them any peaceful alternative.

Paris will continue to be Paris for its revolutionaries. Victor Serge said: "Paris calls us. The Paris of Zola, of the Commune, of the CGT, of the small newspapers printed with burning fervor ... the Paris where Lenin at times edited Iskra and spoke in meetings of small cooperatives filled with immigrants ... the Paris where the headquarters of the Central Committee of the Russian Socialist-Revolutionary Party could be found."

This revolutionary France that has several times opened a Pandora's Box for capitalism in Europe.

This France, that has welcomed so many political refugees and so many revolutionaries, now demands of them today important reflection and an important contribution. It is never too late to begin - or even to begin badly in this way – it just needs to continue.

Those "well-born" people say that the youths - the main protagonists of the disturbances in France today - are not French, but immigrants. It would be good to ask of these "well-born" people and the well positioned bourgeoisie of France, who has the right to sing the Marseillaise – they or the youths of the suburbs? How did the Marseillaise come about? The hymn, one of the revolutionary symbols of the nation, is a hymn that the immigrant youths have as much right to sing as the corrupt French bourgeoisie. The Cuban Bayamesa is the daughter of the Marseillaise. They are more than just nationalist hymns, but revolutionary ones! The Cuban flag, as with so many others of the world, displays its white stripe in honor of those French revolutionaries.

It is true that none of the revolutions in France achieved their goal, but one way or another they all shaped the souls of true revolutionaries. It is never too late to begin again.

I have a 17 year-old son. Of course, what I seek for him is a full life to which a true revolutionary should aspire - that he finds happiness along the diverse road of revolution. But if this cannot be, if we don't manage to build an international Left in a reasonable period of time that will consume his energies and adolescent hormones, I would prefer without any shadow of doubt - rather than seeing him end like Cindy Sheehan's son murdered by the lies of the Empire, killing and being left to die for selfish and merciless interests; before seeing him jumping around in a disco, consuming designer jeans, cars and drugs - without the slightest hesitation, I would prefer to see him setting fire to cars on the streets of Paris.

November, 2005.

Hurricane Reflections

The hurricane season that is now in its last month, has been devastating for our peoples. I believe we were able to go through the entire alphabet assigning names to the tropical depressions, and recently a new one has left Nicaragua named Beta - we are already into the Greek alphabet.

What has happened in these months with natural disasters in this region of the world should force the political, scientific and social leaders of the planet to sit down at a table from which they should not be allowed to leave nor be served any coffee. The Pakistan earthquake, the Southeast Asian tsunami and the heat waves in Europe are, of course, part of this same tragedy. Disasters are not just the privilege of the Caribbean.

In less than a couple of months Katrina, Denis, Rita and Wilma visited us. In the Summit in Mar del Plata we will see of what the presidents speak, although they'd do better to keep their mouths shut and begin listening to what Silvio Rodríguez has to say. It would also be worth them joining the Summit of the Peoples to see if they leave with something intelligible of the world's jigsaw puzzle.

When imperialism first bared its teeth in the Caribbean - when the world almost came to an end in the Cuban Missile crisis in 1962 - nature began to show its disagreement with humankind's administration of this lonely planet.

We sometimes believe that the matter of global warming, and the destruction of the ozone layer are topics for our grandchildren, in a distant future world when maybe we can find another place in the firmament to live... In this selfishness and immaturity, migratory birds seem to take better care of their descendants that our species, which has had the luck to be the only one to write history and the only one to be conscious of its actions.

Ignorance of science is progressively one of the biggest burdens dragging us down - and not only in countries with low educational levels. According to the eminent and now-departed physicist Carl Sagan, the United States is 98% scientifically illiterate. This means not knowing where the demons are located in the Universe, or what our responsibilities are to maintain a minimal ecological balance. And like the drop that overflows the cup, it doesn't end there - Darwin's theory of evolution is now said to be false and his teachings prohibited.

Without turning back, we continue to fall, little by little, into a dark world filled with Middle Ages mystics, witches and black cats, while nature increasingly kills with an irreverent, unprecedented lack of commitment.

That this year is the International Year of Physics, thanks to the great humanist Albert Einstein, is a mere symbol. Science has been scorned from two sides. The rich countries flood us with waste that is incompatible with nature, while we are not able to lower our level of addiction to energy and won't overcome the Freudian ballast of who has the biggest car or house. While all this happens, to quote James Petras: "Bush is a fundamentalist Christian who, rejecting the scientific community, proclaims the biblical history of creationism denigrating the known scientific basis of evolution that is taught in high schools and universities."

If we only change our priorities, the earthquakes and tsunamis and tropical hurricanes that scourge us can become predictable, and we will be have the ability to confront these challenges. The human and economic resources exist, if we leave behind the Crusades, fought in the pathetic name of terrorism.

Carl Sagan said in his book Billions of Billions: "an alien invasion is unlikely, but there is certainly a plethora of common enemies .. They come from our growing technological power and our resistance to doing without short term advantages for the benefit of the long term well-being of our species.

"The innocent act of burning coal and other fossil fuels, increases the warming effect of carbon dioxide and raises the temperature of the Earth ... When the Earth heats, the sea level rises. It's feasible that toward the end of the 21st century it will have risen tens of centimeters, and maybe up to a meter ... Nobody knows when it will happen, but according to the forecasts a time will come when some highly populated islands will be completely submerged ... Devastating effects are also predicted for Venice, Bangkok, Alexandria, New Orleans, Miami, the city of New York and the populous basins of the Mississippi, etc.

"With some population growth, an environment constantly deteriorating and more and more incompetent social systems attempting to deal with rapid change, a new and vast problem will arise: that of environmental refugees ...

"If we continue acting as we do now, the Earth will warm up more every year that passes, droughts as well as floods will become endemic, and many cities, provinces and entire nations will be submerged under the waters unless colossal public works are undertaken to avoid it."

Carl Sagan foretold this in 1996. It was not bravado. We are advocating an ecological crisis that our children, our dogs and our flowers will inherit - to sustain a social system that will put an end to the Earth. It is suicide that is publicized on TV, but is considered to be civilization. I am one of those who think that it is already very late to reason with those who invade us with the contamination of useless products. I am of one of those who think that the modern dragon won't stop at breathing fire unless we cut its head off.

But while we decide if we have the maturity or not to continue inhabiting our beautiful blue planet; while we think of how to rid ourselves of so much cheap Chinese plastic with robot figures that destroy the souls of our children; or to use less polluting perfumes; it is more than ever important to know how to protect ourselves from nature's violence, which will not wait for our tardy reasoning.

Nature respects no national borders. She doesn't wave a flag. Katrina demonstrated before the most incredulous eyes that the omnipotent rulers of the United States also have their South. With proverbial indolence their inept and impotent system called to the inhabitants of the Mississippi basin to "escape and pray." We all saw the babies floating in the waters, we saw the desperation of not knowing where to look, nor where to say to your children: "Here you are safe."

The government of any nation at any time should be ashamed of not having the ability – even if it just be pure information - to protect its citizens. Those of us from poor countries have sometimes been unfair with our brothers and sisters who live in the nations of the North. So, in "Our America", José Martí does not reduce things geographically nor to a single language - there is also a South in the United States, in France and in Australia. With this evident catastrophe comes Karl Marx: the only borders and divisions of our planet are those that divide the exploited from the exploiters. And it was the Blacks and the indigenous of the South who died – the true founders of the country. Ask the Statue of Liberty where she came from and why she came to the U.S. It was a time when the word freedom still meant something.

While we fix the problems of the world which come undone before our eyes, we clearly see the ways of doing things by two different peoples. Several hurricanes have let loose on the small island of Cuba in less than a year. Dennis came a few days before Katrina. The human losses were minimal in spite of ferocious winds. We were able to evacuate more than a million people. None had to "escape" and those who decided to "pray" had already made it to safety. The differences between the economic might of the nations hit by Katrina and Dennis are incomparable. So what happened? Does God love Cubans more? No, although Cubans might respect God, they respect human beings more.

In a recent article published in Rebelión, the Spanish writer Belén Gopegui commented: "not much more than five hundred miles from New Orleans, socialist Cuba, with far fewer resources, has shown it can survive natural disasters with very little or any human loss. Before Hurricane Dennis hit Cuba in July with winds of 240 kilometers per hour - barely 10 kilometers less than the winds of Katrina - more than one and a half million people were evacuated from high risk areas by the island's civil defense network. A million and a half of a total of 11 million inhabitants"

This is not all. After the disaster along the southern coast of the United States, when it seemed that its inhabitants were abandoned to their luck, 1,500 Cubans in white coats organized to travel to New Orleans and the areas affected by Katrina, to help our U.S. brethren. They demanded neither a cent nor a handshake. They were Cuban doctors organized into the Henry Reeve contingent in honor of the U.S. citizen who fought for Cuba's independence.

And they weren't welcome! The sky filled me with tears! Because these people of Louisiana belong to the poor of the world - with those who are left to chance. They refused to accept the more than 1,500 doctors or their medicines. How is this possible? How in the face of waters replete with putrefaction and possible epidemics were doctors not accepted? I don't have enough knowledge of policy to understand this.

You should have seen our doctors, with their white wings like the sea's foam, their backpacks readied and, of course, with Che always with them. The "Inglesito" was the name of the group of doctors trying to do what the President of the United States couldn't do, wouldn't do, nor allow capitalism to pay for. It is doubly murderous not to accept help. The pretext was the money offered to (and refused by) Cubans. Not a single smile of comfort by our young doctors was worth the paltry sum offered!

These young people are now in Pakistan and Honduras. They were also in Mexico. What rich nation is able to offer its youth in this way to countries hit by disaster? How much would be needed to pay doctors trained in the U.S. social system to go to these lost places on the planet? What could we do with the resources dedicated to murdering children in Iraq if this brigade was multiplied by a thousand, by a hundred thousand?

Ah! But not even this is necessary. Let us imagine contingents of scientists like those who made Oppenheimer's atomic bomb which destroyed Japanese cities. Whole contingents, investigating, reducing water temperatures, predicting earthquakes, building cities far from the tsunamis, putting an end to the epidemics that stalk us...making the sky and the sea clearer.

Wilma snatched the color from Havana. Those of us who live on the coast have seen the dead grass and the neighbors who lost everything. Little by little they recover their objects. The green color of my avenue, where I walked some months ago in unrestrained happiness, won't recover easily. The seawater burned the plants as it destroyed the buildings. We are afraid of the force of Nature, but we don't realize the damage we have done to her. It's time to assume a consciousness worthy of the intelligence of our species. The snake has poison, the rose its thorns, and we have reason and the capacity to love each other. The arrogance of believing that we will live forever is unacceptable infantilism. We have only been on the planet a million years, and if we don't adapt to it we won't even leave behind a memory.

Luckily for all, the possible (or not so possible) inhabitants of the Universe, in 1977 Carl Sagan, his partner Ann Druyan, and other scientists sent the Voyager heading for the stars into space at 65,000 km per hour. As Ann Druyan said, the craft "included 60 human languages, the song of a whale, 116 pictures of the Earth, a voice account of our evolution, and 90 minutes of music from a wonderful diversity of the world's cultures. Scientists calculate that these disks of gold could last a billion years."

What other information could we have included? Napalm, enriched uranium, nuclear warheads, AIDS, Katrina, Iraq? I don't think so. Those gold disks take the best of us and just how far we are capable of going. It is better to leave one's dirty washing at home.

Ah! Yes. We should complete one small step if we don't want to end up like the dinosaurs – big for no reason. We should build another society that has already been discovered. Maybe Carl's golden disks are missing the discovery that a classless society is more than possible - it is necessary. That is, if we are to aspire to continue inhabiting the most beautiful and moving place in the Universe.

November, 2005.

"Welcome"... Trotsky

There is a dimension that is lacking in the German film Goodbye Lenin. I know, because I lived in the GDR not long before the Wall came down. This wall was brought down before it was even built. The immense tragedy of the transition to capitalism in Eastern Europe cannot be measured by the few years that elapsed between the vulgar and decadent perestroika and the festive tearing down of statues of Lenin. You cannot say goodbye to Lenin if he was never welcomed. They did nothing but import his image, marginalize him, turn him into a clown subordinated to the Stalinist bureaucracy.

The Lenin to whom they said goodbye in this film had nothing to do with the person who initiated socialism in the world. Their statues were empty of content, and I think, also of form.

So there. We will not understand it as long as the life and ideas of Leon Trotsky remain hidden in many places. It may seem ironic, but the only way to bring Lenin back is to understand the reasons for the banishment of his best contemporary. We will not succeed in understanding what happened if we do not render understandable the obscure mechanism by which the Soviet bureaucratic caste monopolized socialism, betraying the International and demolishing the revolutionary spirit in the world.

Of course there remains an alternative for us: take the mask away entirely, from the beginning, something that will take us time, a thing that is increasingly rare, besides the fact that we lack first-hand information. It is as if, while a ship was sinking, the engineer sent an on-the-spot report on the how and the why of the shipwreck, and that people were nevertheless intending to weigh anchor and head for the same seas with the same intentions, without seeking to know the causes of the catastrophe, burying in the sand, ostrich-like, the message in the bottle.

The 20th century has not finished speaking to us. The vicissitudes that revolutionary practice experienced remain hidden from view. And if there is someone who can be a witness to the 20th century, it is certainly Leon Trotsky.

Ernest Mandel put it much better: "Of all the most important socialists of the 20th century, Trotsky was the one who most clearly recognized the fundamental tendencies of development of the principal contradictions of the epoch, and it is also Trotsky who most clearly formulated an adequate strategy of emancipation for the international workers' movement". [1]

Yes, we need Lenin, who will only come back on condition that we listen to what Trotsky has to say to us. They defended the same thing, except that Trotsky survived him and was able to interpret in his life and in his death the forces that were exterminating socialism. I challenge, at this point in time, any thinker who is sincerely trying to understand what happened, to ignore the experiences of Trotskyism, even if only to refute them. Those who avoid them, those who leave them to one side, are not real Leninists.

They say that without Lenin, Karl Marx is of no use. I would add that without Trotsky there is no Lenin. All the Marxist thinkers, especially genuinely revolutionary Marxists, are indispensable for understanding Karl Marx, who did not have a crystal ball. He only pointed the direction for revolutionary ideas, the philosophy, so that for the first time in history people could dig the tunnel towards their - globalized - happiness.

Let us use this simile. Socialism is supposed to be a tunnel, a path that we can take, in this world where we have only things to win and nothing to lose but our chains. Well, it was the October Revolution that was the first attempt to dig this tunnel that Marx told us about.

But Stalinism dynamited it from within. When it was being built, dynamite had been left to destroy it. Trotsky was the engineer who showed where the explosives were. They didn't want to listen to him. We know what happened then... the planet Earth was ravaged.

Today we declare very poetically that the tunnel we are going to build will be the socialism of the 21st century. Whether it is of the 21st or the 31st century, the tunnel can be dynamited because of exactly the same insufficiencies and we will continue, full of tears, waiting for the socialism of the future century...this time turned into cockroaches.

The possibility of a transition to socialism is a scientific discovery. It is not a poem or a way of speaking. The only way to get there is through the class struggle. It's as simple as that.

The discovery of the origin of capitalist exploitation is a scientific truth of the same value and the same objectivity as the rotating movement of the earth around the sun. We don't need Einstein, the Laws of General Relativity and of Geodesy to explain to us why we go from summer to autumn. Newton is more than sufficient. The results are identical and the mathematics are infinitely more simple.

We don't need to understand black holes or Hawking's theories to put a satellite into orbit. It may be that communications, computers and so on have somewhat complicated the reality of modern capitalism, but it nonetheless remains true that the essence (the "chicken" in the "rice and chicken") is still the same as several centuries ago. There is no need for "quantum economists" or "tensorial mathematics" to explain to us the origin of the exploitation of the capitalist system and its present weakening.

What we call "socialism of the 21st century" amounts to saying that we have to build "the aeroplane of the 21st century". But this plane will have to overcome gravity, just as the plane of the 20th century did. In this 21st century, as for millions of years, the constant G of Universal Gravitation is still the one that Newton calculated ($G = 6.7 \times 10^{-11} m3/kgs2$).

I admit that we have to make more comfortable, faster and more secure aeroplanes, because the demands of the 21st century are different from those of the 20th century, but the ultimate reason for a machine that has to conquer gravity is the same.

By way of comparison, we could say that our plane, which tried to conquer gravity in 1917, took off and crashed on the earth's surface. It would be better to look for the causes before engaging in nay futuristic discourses, because whatever the 21st century is, G remains invariable. From the 19th to the 21st century, the primary causes of capitalist exploitation are identical: the expropriation of labor. So there is only one way to go "from the reign of necessity to the reign of liberty". Enough of cutting capers, when each instant that passes counts against us.

The plane fell, and now we believe that with our computers, our cellphones or the internet we are going to be able to defy gravity without taking G into account. Of course not! Gravity will continue in the same way until the planet disintegrates. We had better get a move on, drop the rhetoric and realize once and for all that the enemy has not changed. He is perhaps more aggressive and dangerous, but still the same. Let us hurry, at last, to find out who we really are.

But why then Leon Trotsky? I don't have a fixation with a historical figure, as many people reproach me with having. It's just that this man knew a lot of things about the black box of this plane that wanted to make history take off.

Leon Trotsky was assassinated 65 years ago, in the most grotesque manner. After 65 years, we are still spattered by his blood. This assassination ought to have put an end to the Kremlin's right to try and monopolize and transmit socialist thought, but they continued and it became transformed into a salt statue.

With the Red Star medal awarded to Ramon Mercader, they celebrated, with secret and cowardly hurrahs, the death of socialism. This assassination was one of the most perverse terrorist acts in history. It was the glorious October 1917 that committed suicide on August 20th.

Mercader, having served his sentence in Mexico, went to Cuba (in 1960). I still don't understand who he met and how, nor if he could look in the face Marti's crown of martyrdom and Mella's ashes. The man who had in his hands, without realizing it, the mission of wiping out the left wing of socialist ideas, died in Cuba, something I have difficulty in coming to terms with. He was there in those luminous years of Che Guevara. That seems to me so impossible ...

Of course the road of the ideological survival of the Cuban Revolution had nothing to do with Mercader, the GPU and Stalinism. Quite to the contrary, what enabled my revolution to survive was the spirit of Leon Trotsky, although we didn't know it, because it had been hidden in the folds of historical memory. The truth is stubborn and it makes its way like slow but constant water that nothing can stop.

There is a mysterious circuit in the Cuban Revolution, which was born with the Cuban Revolutionary Party, continued with Mella, then with the most radical wing of the July 26th Movement, culminating in a sublime way with Che Guevara. This is the circuit of resolute class commitment and internationalism.

Leon Trotsky walks here, silent, unknown and slandered, with a malicious smile. Why was it forbidden for so many years to put Leon Trotsky in relation with the Cuban Revolution? I haven't managed to find out, but I know that if there is a revolution that has been radical, it is certainly ours. And if there was someone who called for revolutions that were radical and never-ending, it was certainly Leon Trotsky. Perhaps Marti was not mistaken when he declared that "in politics the real is what is not seen".

We should speak at length of Julio Antonio Mella and analyze in depth his activity in Mexico. Fortunately we have the excellent works of Olivia Gall [2] and Alejandro Galvez Cancino, [3] which analyze in an absolutely clear and precise fashion, with considerable documentation, the communist activity of Mella in this period.

Mella referred to Trotsky after returning from the USSR and knew the objectives of the Left Opposition through Andreu Nin (assassinated, just for a change, by the GPU during the Spanish Civil War). He wrote to a comrade in the book The Platform of the Left Opposition: "For Alberto Martinez, with the aim of rearming communism. Julio Antonio Mella". [4] His declared Trotskyism is not what should be most important for us. Much more transcendent were his radical positions in Mexico. In fact, and in his political consequences, "Mella is considered by the Trotskyists as the initiator of the current that later constituted the Left Opposition in the Mexican Communist Party", says the historian Olivia Gall. [5]

It was also Julio Antonio Mella who introduced us to the road to socialism in Cuba. It was he who established the superb bridge between Marti and Bolshevism, which represents the best of our recent past and the near future of the world. Whatever might be said, and even if some people would like to wrap him up in a pathetic patriotic flag and attribute a narrow discourse to him, this valiant, vigorous and polemical Mella - and no other - was the first Cuban communist.

The Stalinism which subsequently contaminated us, and which in a certain fashion had its importance during the course of the socialist revolution, is nothing other than a contagious virus, in spite of which, and not without battles, the ideal of socialism was able to survive, because it was the very essence of the revolutionary process. The Stalinist parties did not contribute ideologically to our process, neither when they expelled Mella from the party, nor when they collaborated with Machado, or any many other occasions, thank God!

There are still some comrades here who have a lot to tell us, faithful to the socialist revolution...and grateful to have been helped and listened to by another Marxist who figures alongside Mella on the emblem of the Union of Communist Youth of Cuba: Che.

And it is precisely Che that I want to invite, in his totality and with the star on his forehead, to extend a welcome to Trotsky on this 65th anniversary of his assassination. Che Guevara, symbol of the most radical communism, managed to fashion an instrument out of a Trotskyism that he didn't know. And that was only because the theoretical truths of Trotsky have the same constancy as the value of G, the constant of Universal Gravitation. Che found his own way to many of Trotsky's theses, without ever knowing it...without being allowed to know it.

I am going to give two examples which enabled me to begin to discover a secret communion between the two of them.

Che Guevara was the revolutionary who best understood the principles of the permanent revolution, to such an extent that he died for having tried to defend these principles. But he not only died for having wanted to implement these theses, he also died for having sought, intellectually, to reach its essence.

For this 65th anniversary I am going to take up again here the three fundamental aspects of the permanent revolution.

First aspect: "The theory of the permanent revolution, which originated in 1905, declared war upon these ideas and moods. It pointed out that the democratic tasks of the backward bourgeois nations lead directly, in our epoch, to the dictatorship of the proletariat and that the dictatorship of the proletariat puts socialist tasks on the order of the day." [6].

Che was categorical on this subject. Here is what Nestor Kohan has to say about it:

"He (Che) at no time accepted that in Latin America (I would add: and in the world) the tasks consist of building a "national revolution", "democratic", "progressive", or a capitalism with a human face, which leaves socialism till later. He expounds in a trenchant fashion, very polemical, that if we do not propose to make the socialist revolution, then what results is a caricature of revolution, or ends in failure or tragedy, as has happened so many times." [7]

These two exposés are identical. The underdeveloped countries don't have to wait till an English or German person decides to organize the revolution in their countries. Trotsky said that, in the Manifesto of the Conference known as the "emergency" conference of the Fourth International in May 1940:

"The perspective of the permanent revolution in no case signifies that the backward countries must await the signal from the advanced ones, or that the colonial peoples should patiently wait for the proletariat of the metropolitan centers to free them. Help comes to those who helps themselves."

In its second aspect, "The second aspect of the 'permanent' theory has to do with the socialist revolution as such. For an indefinitely long time and in constant internal struggle, all social relations undergo transformation. Society keeps on changing its skin. ... Revolutions in economy, technique, science, the family, morals and everyday life develop in complex reciprocal action and do not allow society to achieve equilibrium. Therein lies the permanent character of the socialist revolution as such." [8]

For his part, Che wrote in Socialism and Man in Cuba:

"In this period of the building of socialism we can see the birth of the new man. His image is not yet quite fixed. It will never be able to be, given that the process is parallel to the development of new economic structures." [9]

For Che, "the only rest for revolutionaries is the tomb".

Third aspect: international. For Trotsky:

"The international character of the socialist revolution, which constitutes the third aspect of the theory of the permanent revolution, flows from the present state of economy and the social structure of humanity. Internationalism is no abstract principle but a theoretical and political reflection of the character of world economy, of the world development of productive forces and the world scale of the class struggle. The socialist revolution begins on national foundations-but it cannot be completed within these foundations. The maintenance of the proletarian revolution within a national framework can only be a provisional state of affairs, even though, as the experience of the Soviet Union shows, one of long duration. In an isolated proletarian dictatorship, the internal and external contradictions grow inevitably along with the successes achieved. If it remains isolated, the proletarian state must finally fall victim to these contradictions." [10]

Che said on the subject of revolutionaries:

"If their revolutionary ardor dulls when the most pressing tasks have to be carried out at the local level and proletarian internationalism is forgotten, then the revolution ceases to be a driving force and falls into a gentle somnolence, of which our irreconcilable enemy, imperialism, takes advantage to gain ground. Internationalism is a duty, but also a revolutionary necessity." [11]

I will not waste time. If there is someone who always fought to make the Cuban Revolution ever more socialist, it was Che. He threw himself into the building of socialism in a backward land, deepening day after day its socialist character...only to completely abandon it in the name of the world revolution. I do not know anyone else who did the same. I don't think there is any greater fidelity to the theses of the permanent revolution. That the conditions in Bolivia were not favorable...that is another subject than the permanent revolution. We can certainly criticize him for having been too permanent or too consistent a revolutionary.

The other element of convergence, in different circumstances, between Trotsky's thought and Che's, resides in their firm commitment to planned economy. It is certain that Trotsky initially opted for the NEP, given the terrible economic circumstances in which the young Soviet state found itself with what was known as War Communism.

But Trotsky very quickly criticized the new state of affairs. He considered, as Isaac Deutscher describes to us, that

"with the move to the NEP, the necessity of planning became more urgent (...) Precisely because the country was reviving under a market economy, it was necessary to see that the market was controlled, and to have the means of exercising this control. He went on to raise the question of the Single Plan, without which it was impossible to rationalize production, to concentrate industrial resources and to establish equilibrium between the different sectors of the economy." [12]

Che's positions in favor of the plan and his proverbial aversion to the NEP are well known. Che considered that Lenin, if he had had the time, would have revised his opinion of the NEP. And there was not only the plan. Che also took a position, at the end oh his life, in favor of socialist democracy. Michael Lowy writes in Rebelión:

"We know that in the last years of his life Ernesto Che Guevara had made considerable progress in distancing himself from the Soviet paradigm (...) But a large part of his later writings still remains unpublished, for inexplicable reasons. Among these documents there is a radical critique of the Manual of Political Economy of the Academy of Sciences of the USSR, written in Prague in 1966 (...) One of its passages is very interesting, because it demonstrates that in his later political thinking, Guevara was coming round to the idea of socialist democracy." [13]

That was what Che was like. Although he had insufficiently studied Leon Trotsky, he was going in the direction of the most consistent Trotskyist theses. Perhaps he wasn't conscious of it, but that is of little importance. It indicates in any case that these theses are correct and in return gives even more force to Trotsky's thought. In 1965, Che wrote to Armando Hart from Tanzania about his choices concerning Marxist philosophy, and in paragraph VII he told him: "And we should find there your friend Trotsky, who it seems existed and wrote." [14]

That may make us think that he didn't know a lot about the founder of the Red Army. It appears nevertheless that during the last year of his life he drew closer to his works. Juan Leon Ferrer, a Trotskyist comrade who worked in the Ministry of Industry, assured me of this. Furthermore, Che received the periodical of his organization, and it was Che who had the imprisoned Trotskyists freed on his return from Africa. Comrade Roberto Acosta, who has since died, shared a close comradeship with

Guevara. According to Jose Leon Ferrer, during the sugar harvests (zafras), they spoke of these subjects. This comrade says that Che had read Permanent Revolution, and we know that in Bolivia he was carrying in his backpack the History of the Russian Revolution.

We could add many examples which show that these two exemplary revolutionaries lit up the same path.

Both of them brilliantly and successfully led an army and a nascent socialist state, fully applying the teachings of Karl Marx; both of them were revolutionary ideologues who took power and sought to deepen the revolutionary process while remaining, respectively, loyal to Lenin and Fidel, leaning to their left. For representing the most developed ideal of internationalism and revolutionary consistency, both were assassinated.

Ernesto Guevara made me a Trotskyist. When I had access to Trotsky's writings, very belatedly for my liking, I realized that many things had already been told to me from my childhood onwards, by Che. From the first pages, I had the confirmation of what I had so many times felt in reading Che: that the revolution has nothing to do with national idiosyncrasy; that there is no room in socialism for the pronouns "our" or "your"; that revolutionary theory, like the laws of physics, is a universal language.

As Armando Hart stated in another epoch:

"Our struggle is not only for Cuba, but for all the workers and the exploited of the world. Our frontiers are moral. Our limits are those of class." [15]

What I most appreciate in Trotsky is his way of speaking, the passion that his discourses always awaken in me. It is the same thing that subjugated me with Che Guevara. That is why I am fighting in his army, as in Che's, without betraying anyone. Both of them express with the same truth the word, the gun and the heart.

Comrades: let us finally come of age. There is too much injustice, too much exploitation, the evidence of the unique solution is only too great; too many of ours are dead. Leon Trotsky is calling us back to the struggle. Let us bid him unconditionally welcome!

Che Guevara is his amphytron, and the peoples of Latin America are demanding socialism. Trotsky has won the theoretical match in a dramatic way. Let us without delay and with confidence arm our revolutionary movements. Trotsky and Che are in our party. Let us once and for all give the tree a good shake, so as to unmask the new reformists who are preventing the Bolivarian revolution from advancing - this revolution which is the spearhead, the first rung on the ladder of an unprecedented continental revolution.

Let us remember once again that the sun, the stars and gravity are our allies. Workers of all lands, unite!

Published in International Viewpoint, October, 2005.

NOTES

[1] Ernest Mandel: Trotsky as Alternative, London, Verso, 1995.
[2] Olivia Gall: Trotsky en Mexico, Coleccion Problemas de Mexico, 1991. Olivia's Gall's doctoral thesis (in French), Trotsky et la vie politique dans le Mexique de Cardenas (Université de Grenoble 2, 1986) is also essential reading.
[3] Alejandro Galvez Cancino: Julio Antonio Mella. Un marxista revolucionario, Critica de l'Economia Politica, 1986.
[4] Ibid.
[5] Olivia Gall, op. cit.
[6] Leon Trotsky, The Permanent Revolution, 1931 Introduction to the Russian edition 1929, available on www.marxists.org
[7] Nestor Kohan: Ernesto Che Guevara. Otro mundo es posible, Editorial Nuestra America, 2003.
[8] Trotsky, op. cit.
[9] Ernesto Guevara: Socialism and Man in Cuba.
[10] Trotsky, op. cit.
[11] Guevara, op. cit.
[12] Isaac Deutscher, The Prophet Unarmed.
[13] Michael Lowy, "Ni calco ni copia: Che Guevara en busqueda de un nuevo socialismo ". Rebelión, August 5th, 2002. (Publisher's note -- The writings Lowy refers to were published only in 2006, under the tirle *Apuntes Críticos a la Economía Política*).
[14] Ernesto Guevara, Letter of December 4th, 1965 to Armando Hart, published in 1997 by the Cuban journal Contracorriente. In his book mentioned in note 7 above, Nestor Kohan presents and analyses this letter, which remained unpublished for over 30 years.
[15] Armando Hart "Greetings from the Central Committee of the Cuban Communist Party to the 23rd Congress of the Communist Party of the Soviet Union". (Published in Politica internacional de la Revolucion Cubana, Editora Politica, 1966).

The Last Flight of the Santamarías

In the most difficult days of the clandestine struggle, our last battle to become free; when there were not enough contacts, or safe houses to hide in; as we faced the most brutal threats from a tyranny that was losing its battle and kept murdering the best young people in the country, there floated in the streets of Havana, a subtle, graceful and beautiful woman, with white hair and the strongest of looks from the darkest of eyes.

My aunt Aida Santamaría was the most serene and beautiful of the strange and emblematic Santamarías that gave their hearts to the Cuban Revolution. When Chaviano [one of Batista's most feared henchmen] learnt she was visiting the jail or making legal arrangements he would always be at a loss and not knowing what to do to a woman of such beauty and serenity, would only repeat like an idiot, "Oh, the little white dove, the little white dove!"

In the same way Haydée had an overflowing passion and an intelligence molded by emotions; in the same way uncle Aldo represented courage – someone who was entrusted with the secret of the landing of the Granma expedition and the secret of the strategic missiles during the Caribbean Crisis [known in Cuba as the October Missile Crisis of 1962]; in that same way little Aidita was the symbol of joy, of art. At her house of endless partying, Silvio and Pablo [Silvio Rodríguez and Pablo Milanés, Cuban trovadores and songwriters] found their best audiences. In the same way that, lastly… or rather firstly, Abel was the symbol of absolute dedication – an immaculate saint of green eyes; eyes with which our enemies wanted to buy my mother's heart in the jails of Santiago de Cuba— Aida Santamaría whom we have just buried, was the symbol of serenity, of coherence. She was the kind of person everyone would go to when they needed to deal with a problem. It is said that when it became obvious that the little white dove was the most committed of the revolutionaries and she was ordered by agents of the tyranny in Encrucijada (hometown of the Santamarías) to leave the country, these agents found in a bookcase a book that had been taken there by orders of Fidel. A book Fidel knew was already part of History. One of the agents looked at the book signed by uncle Abel and, half surprised half threatening, said, "Abel, he's the one who died in Moncada" and aunt Aida, undisturbed, answered, "No, Abel was the one who was murdered in a cowardly way in Moncada." It is said the agent looked at my aunt questioningly, but her beautiful eyes looked steadily at the man's face for a long while. The henchman put the book back in the bookcase, in the same way the devil fears the cross.

At the triumph of the Cuban Revolution, which received as a legacy the life of her brother Abel and the sorrow of her family, Aida devoted herself entirely to the new tasks.

She headed the Departmento de Prevención y Asistencia Social [Social Work Directorate]. Social workers who are now our pride, had their first job under the wings of this little white dove who after January '59 decided to fly much higher.

Funeral parlors. slums, war veterans were objects of her attention. She was our first social worker. Goods and property left behind by the killers and cowards that fled the country were distributed among the needy by her white hands.

I remember that when I was a child during the sugar harvest in 1970 my parents were in Amancio Rodriguez, a little fishermen village in the province of Camaguey. As my father encouraged the cane cutters to reach the goal of the 10 million tons of sugar – and by the way, if we had reached the goal many problems would have been avoided, because the price we paid for the "defeat" of not reaching the goal was to fall into the hands of the Soviet bureaucracy with its many aberrations – well, as Armando Hart encouraged and organized the production of sugar, my mother was in charge of building a road, a water duct and other works in "Macondo" as she had renamed the village. She distributed bricks for peasant houses and social buildings. Then, like in a fairy tale, my aunt Aida would send down many goods left behind by the bourgeois who were leaving the country in a hurry: The farmers in Amancio Rodriguez got, together with their cane cutting job, quality pots and pans, fine cutlery, luxury bed linen, all sent from Aida Santamaria's Department of Recovered Goods. Not that this was important for the humble to understand the Revolution, but somehow it was a sign of the times that the morning coffee of the cane cutters was served in a container that had once belonged to an embezzler or a thief. And these objects had not changed hands from defeated thieves to thieves in power: They were now in the hands of the people, of those who did not care if the china they used had this or that fine American brand, they would continue drinking their coffee for the "ten million ton harvest" oblivious of the containers and the mediocre and wasteful banana republic bourgeoisie that had left them behind.

Aida remained the stronghold in her family, mediator in the fights between my grandmother Joaquina and my mother; midwife (to call it somehow) of all her nephews. My mother used to tell me that when I decided to be born, it was not still time, because Aida had not yet arrived. To come into this world I had to wait for the approval and aplomb of my aunt Aida.

She died a Communist Party militant, trying to have us all, her sons, daughters and nephews, who grew up in the blessed Santamaría maelstrom, remain loyal to these commitments.

As was her duty, Aida buried her four brothers and sisters. Which was the most painful? One was murdered, another committed suicide, the youngest died before her time suffering from a consuming cancer... My uncle Aldo a year ago in the same way...

She stood by their graves and tried to ease the confused and different sorrows of their descendants.

This can be the end, at least for us: The last branch of this miracle tree has returned to earth.

I don't know if my cousins, my brother, and I have inherited some of their magic, but it will not bloom in the same way: we are contaminated by new times, new urgencies and much less love.

An extended chapter of this peculiar work of the Revolution was closed today.

Let's hold our hands with fervor... and... thought...and much love so that the pure ashes of that legion of enlightened beings walk with us a little further, when we have to cope with death in the years we still have. I don't believe magic ever dies, but today at least I have lost my faith to try to find it.

With today's burial something very beautiful and intangible has finally ended in the luminous history of a revolution, made of angel feathers.

February, 2005.

A butterfly against Stalin: the 25th Anniversary of the Death of Celia Sanchez Manduley

In Cuba, bureaucracy encountered a unique adversary. Celia Sánchez, Fidel Castro's secretary, had not read much about Marxist theory in her life or about the part played by Stalin in the USSR. She was, however, a corrective force against the practice, in Cuba, of the methods of that Georgian [Stalin], which to this day have given us so much to talk about and to do.

Celia, to whom I owe the beautiful sound of my name, was not only the personal secretary of Fidel, renouncing everything: family, political visibility, and other benefits she deserved for being the first woman rebel in the Sierra Maestra. Celia was, in fact, the personal secretary of the Cuban revolution. She was the first lady, but not the first lady of the Republic of Cuba. She was decidedly the first rebel woman of the Cuban socialist revolution.

Celia set up a bridge between Fidel and the people, a light and flexible bridge. Her wisdom and briskness, her light step, her quietness, and her love for the revolution, to which she was so devoted—those were her best weapons. Freeing myself from any sense of machismo or feminism or any other isms they can assign to me, I envision José Martí thinking of Celia Sánchez when he wrote: "It is not that she is lacking any of the best capacities a man has, but that her fine and sensitive nature sends her to higher and more difficult tasks."

As a child, Celia and her father, a physician working in Manzanillo, his home town, took a bust of Martí to the highest point in the island. Thus the initiation of Cuban revolutionaries is recorded together with the name José Martí. If the words of this mystery are felt rather than understood as a child, nothing more needs to be said; you will become a revolutionary. And if you betray this, nothing more can be done to prevent you from becoming the worst of/human beings. In her fragile structure, her thin hands, and the colors of her unique clothing, José Martí, Fidel Castro, and the Cuban people were joined without clashing. To know about Celia it is enough to look at the beautiful book *Ensayo para una biografía* (Essay for a biography) by Pedro Alvarez Tabío.

Celia Sánchez Manduley was born in May 1920, in Media Luna, a small rural town with about 4,000 inhabitants in Oriente province (the eastern part of the island) near the Vicana River, which has its source in the Sierra Maestra, no more, no less.

If anything can be said of the place, Media Luna worked in the production of sugar, which was low in 1920; when several workers strikes took place; and when the auspicious Socialist Party, founded in 1906 by Martín Velóz (Martinillo), was already spreading socialist ideas in Manzanillo, during the first decade of the century. If we add to this the undaunted devotion to José Martí and to the history of Cuba felt by her father, Manuel Sánchez, along with an intrepid genetics, Celia could not have been different.

Armando Hart writes in his essay "Profiles": "I remember the first time I heard talk of Celia (1950). The comrades Pedro Miret and Nico López went to Santiago to make contact with Frank País, to tour around Oriente province and analyze the probable areas we could use as locations for revolutionary combat …They returned to Havana from Oriente, happy with the possibilities they had found in Manzanillo, where Celia and other comrades organized clandestine cells and supported the popular movement against the tyranny."

At some time we will have to stop and calibrate Cuban society then …

Fidel Castro must have been a great man for being able to sum up, organize, and launch as only one revolutionary party the many and formidable forces existing in my country.

In 1957 Celia made the transition definitively to working with Fidel. From that moment on she turned over the spirit of the people that she carried within her to the immensity of Fidel, being present at every decision and giving that same audacity, tenderness, and commitment with which she placed the first bust of Martí in the Pico Turquino. Celia Sánchez placed her gifts of revolutionary, guerrilla, and organizer in the hands of Fidel Castro who, after that, could no longer leave behind that slender military strategist.

Once the revolution triumphed, her mission was the same: that of transducer. A perfect mediator between the work of the revolution, its people, and its leaders.

I remember, as a child, that my father would say: "I'm going to go see Celia.". He said it like a sacred act, partially secret, as if he was going to confession. And that was true: facing Celia who had the magical power to join heaven and earth without showing off, like ideas and sublime projects that she transformed into rapid memos, efficient meetings, and pertinent engagements. The administrative life of Fidel Castro: The impressive Agrarian Reform, the Declarations of Havana, Girón—and the October Crisis, when the world was about to end in a nuclear war—somehow all these were weighed and decided in a building on 11th Street in the neighborhood of Vedado in the capital. There Celia and Fidel lived, each in their own apartment, like good neighbors.

My mother and Celia formed a sort of revolutionary sisterhood. The intuition in face of the problems, the character of the comrades, everything was settled by these two women as if they were still making a revolution. And they were! They were the revolutionaries who lasted through time, the ones who did not betray, those who did not abandon us either politically or economically—which is also a form of betrayal. They are there today, in combat. They are the ones who still suffer when they encounter negligence; who, wherever they are, do not hesitate to stop and ask and question and change. Because the revolution that Celia planned together with Fidel, Frank, Che, Camilo, Haydée, [and others] is absolutely the only revolution possible in Cuba and in the world. And that revolution is permanent. Celia was a permanent revolutionary. For this reason only we remember her 25 years after her death. Because we need Celia Sánchez.

Recently I uselessly tried to make myself understood by a comrade about the elements of Stalinist bureaucracy in the Cuban revolution. I tried to explain how this revolution lived its first fifteen years without becoming institutionalized, how tasks of prime importance were pushed forward, with that heterodox form, such as the literacy campaign, the educational plans, and all the reforms that, more than reforms, are revolutions or missions that made this revolution the dream of millions of young men and women in the world, that perfectly organized the political life of Cuba.

The triumphant socialist revolutions must conquer a subtle and persistent and ... *deep-rooted*... enemy. Stalinism. Stalinism (to somehow give a name to this tendency) can do away with the resolves of socialism. The danger of trying to keep alive the socialist revolution and not try, uselessly, to build socialism in only one country, the agony of always being alone...or of having strange bedfellows; such things infect us with this disease, which is mortal if not caught in time, but easy to cure if we have hearts, intelligence, and courage in serving the revolution, as Celia showed. Stalinism with its resort to dark and widespread abuse of power, its contract with political mediocrity, its hatred for talent and adventure is a destructive power like the bacteria that defeated the Martians in the renowned work written by H. G. Wells and broadcast by Orson Welles—"The War of the Worlds."

Neither science nor the highest skills and will of men could destroy them. Merely some minute organisms were able to wipe out these invaders from space. That is the way Stalinism works. No, but don't think I am a pessimist: We are hit by bacteria and acquire bacteria every day. But we also have lymphocytes. They protect us from disease in this battle. If the macrophages cannot handle it, if there are too many bacteria or if they are very new, it's enough to attack them with the right antibiotic and in a few days we are saved. Stalinism is a bacterium we acquire when we achieve power. But, we also have many good bacteria that we didn't have before. With Stalinism it's enough to be vaccinated periodically.

The socialist revolution, being a new form of power needs new vaccines. We spend time being careful about "accidents" or foreign "aggressors" and do not take care to be vaccinated against self-generating ills. This has been one of the problems of revolutions ... A vaccine, a simple vaccine. There are moments when it is too late and we must apply drips with strong antibiotics that are drastic measures, those that are a two-edged sword, but necessary.

"It would be naïve to think that Stalin, unknown by the masses, suddenly rose up from the background armed with a strategic plan all prepared. No ... Before he had set out on his road, bureaucracy had predicted him ...", Trotsky said ("The revolution betrayed"). In my opinion, Trotsky has always given the best diagnosis of the disease. That is Stalin: he was the repository of that natural stress that a socialist revolution undergoes. Even more so if it is a socialist revolution that is isolated and persecuted by a fierce imperialism. The invisible siege of Stalinism is much more dangerous then.

One of these vaccines, one that fought this bacterium in my revolution, naturally and organically, was Celia Sánchez. She never lost the bonds with the people. The harder the international political scene, the more she boosted popular opinion.

In Cuba, Lenin has not died, and this is a new experience, a form of salvation. But in the early years when the revolution was an infant, then the arms of Celia lulled it through her devotion to the truth, her incredible practical sense, and her deep knowledge of the personality of

Fidel and the rest of the leaders of the revolution. She fulfilled her task of protecting them from the assaults of Stalinism, which was of course translated from Russian to our Spanish. I don't know if Celia had read about the Bolshevik revolution. It doesn't matter; her instinct added, of course, to the impact of Fidel, the audacity of Che, and the mental structure of this people that saved the newborn.

In 1975 the first Congress of the Party and its institutionalization occurred. Armando Hart again says: "The guerrilla fighter of the mountains of Oriente, she who liked to sleep in hammocks and walk along the trails...was, however, capable of promoting, organizing, and finding her way amid the formalities of the official tasks that all states inevitably have."

It was another stage of the revolution. Left behind were many things. The young revolution dressed in long gowns; she was 15 years old. Celia knew how to rise to the occasion and understand the road and somehow solve the new circumstances around her ... this young woman. She enjoyed the beautiful: she enjoyed and cultivated it like the mariposa flower.

I still don't understand how these two women who never went to university were the masters of beauty in Cuba. My mother in the Casa de las Americas with the irreverent intellectuals of this country and Celia in the mystical ambiance of Fidel Castro. I have a clear memory of the Summit Meeting of Non-Aligned Nations in 1979. Celia displayed a fine sense of taste in the uniforms of the waitresses, the housing provided for the invited heads of state, the meals, and the cocktails. Everything had a tropical flavor with light and clarity without excess, maintaining the strictest etiquette. She designed everything, from the beautiful reception hall of the Council of State, where still, they say, the giant ferns sway, to the rocks that are still in the majestic and popular Lenin Park.

Perhaps her love of beauty made her a true revolutionary and could frighten off the dark ghost of Stalin, that gray ghost that has always wanted to swallow up the infinite light of that authentic [and good] "specter" mentioned in the first line of the Communist Manifesto. Or perhaps she could enhance and harmonize the life of Fidel just because she was a true revolutionary. It's the famous story of the chicken and the egg. It doesn't matter. One thing is clear for us: Somehow Celia was the summary of the people of Cuba, not of a particular woman or man, but the best part of the Cuban people. She never stopped being a woman of the people, delicate and pure, who also wielded power.

Che reminded us endlessly that one of our sacred duties was world revolution. Celia, with her rapid gait reminded us to never stop the revolution within our watery borders. Better advice? Impossible!

The many Vietnams in America are the simple solution to the problems of the world, although so many Congresses and useless rhetoric want to complicate it. Today, to fight against that serial assassin that is the government of the United States and its allies has become the common goal for communists, Muslims, Christians, if they are all authentic. It is beautiful to say that the socialist revolution is the only savior of Christianity and other religions (I want to list them but I don't know all those isms). This monster [Bush] has no pity. And, little by little, but assuredly, he is approaching Hitler. Perhaps his new team can help him write *Mein Kampf.* The world is getting desperate. The tsunami in

Southeast Asia could not be prevented, but we know well that if the sensors of seismic movements had been put in place, as they were elsewhere, lives could have been saved. If only Bush et al., who are so Christian, remembered the commandment "Thou shalt not kill," it would save both bullets and bodies. Then we would know a lot more that is hidden from us now by the stupidity of power and money. And after the triumph over this monster there is the loving care of Celia. It's as simple as that.

Celia was implacable with imperialism and the enemies of the Cuban revolution, who are, all told, the enemies of the world. She didn't permit, for one instant, the shroud of bureaucracy to cloud the task at hand. She could not save us from all its manifestation, but at least she knew the enemy, because Stalinism is also our enemy. She knew that while she lived alongside Fidel she would give it no space. There were, undoubtedly, Stalinist tendencies. There is a tendency for that which is bureaucratic to subtly penetrate society and for that which is mediocre to find followers, but in Celia this tendency encountered its most hardened opponent.

I remember as if today were January 9, 1980. Haydée Santamaria got us out of bed, just this once. They say that the only time they saw her in that state was in 1967 with the death of Che. Amid constant tears I heard mi mother say only one word that made her cry more: "*Fidel,* my daughter. Who will take care of *Fidel* now?" "Fidel is healthy, Mama. There are many comrades taking care of him," I answered. But today I understand my mother. With Celia the people took care of Fidel, its best comrade.

It is twenty-five years now that these two women have no longer been with us. So many things have ceased to exist! Now the USSR is not threatening us with its oil, its cement, its protection, but the double economy in my homeland is dancing, and I don't know if there is a way to free ourselves from this economic artifact that the double currency represents and brings with it. Imperialism we combat with weapons and ideas. It seems that to care for ourselves against these new evils we need the "mariposa," the butterfly...

Every morning when I take my son to school I observe those fragile and willful winged beings that, in unequaled flight, enfold us. I wonder if Celia remembered, before dying, to explain to these little ladies how much we need them to protect us from the new ghosts.

Published by Labor Standard, January, 2005.

"We are always living the Revolution in Cuba."

The compañera analyzes the current situation in the island, the challenges facing her every day, and current Socialist and revolutionary ideas.
Daughter of two Cuban revolutionaries, Armando Hart and Haydee Santamaría, soon after receiving her Ph.D. in Physics, Celia Hart Santamaría decided that she wanted to work doing something else. "I involved myself entirely in my passion: the Revolution, from an international perspective," the compañera states as an introduction.

"God punished me for being born in the only country in the entire world where you cannot belong to the opposition, because the government itself is the opposition, which always disconcerted me a little bit. I am in Cuba, which is the opposition in the world, and that consoles me," she explains. She remembers her mother, one of the two women who participated in the Moncada attack in 1953, as a person with an "overwhelming passion."

Celia currently works in the Museo Santamaría, located in the same apartment which her uncle Abel and her mother left one day to become the main figures in the Moncada attack. A similar episode took place over there [1]. "My uncle Abel had gotten together a group of Juventud Ortodoxa (Youth from the Orthodox Party), later he was introduced to Fidel, then my uncle told my mom that he knew already who the leader of the revolution was going to be, she told him `you,' but he was already thinking about Fidel. And my mother, mad with Fidel, because he was getting the floor dirty with tobacco...," she recalls, smiling.

Q: How is the relationship between the new Cuban generations and the Revolution?

A: The Revolution is won mainly by winning the youth over. Youth is intrinsically authentically socialist, but sometimes, because of our limitations, we do something and youth loses that spirit. As a member of the Cuban Communist Party, I am concerned about some of the issues that Cuban and World Communists must resolve. Besides being in power and in the government, the Cuban Revolution must always continue being a revolution, in spite of the fact that every state, including the dictatorship of the proletariat, has a tendency to become conservative. Fortunately, Fidel is always revolutionizing things.

Starting with the case of Elian Gonzalez, there was a clue that we are still alive, because it would be very sad that the Moncadistas were the only heroes. Now we have our five heroes locked up in the United States, who are renewing us. Now we do not have to appeal only to my uncle Abel, or to Che, or to so many dead comrades, but we have five heroes to fight for. The most important challenge for us, communists, besides freeing our comrades, is giving that to our youth, so they feel that there are five heroes, five comrades our age, struggling against Yankee imperialism, because they, from inside prison, are struggling.

Besides anti-terrorist fighters, taking into account that the Miami mafia is an accomplice of the U.S. Government, they fight against imperialism, therefore, they are internationalists.

Our greatest challenge is to give our flag to our youth, so they take it as their own, those heroes belong to them.

Q: Then, what is the message for youth?

A: The youth must be told that the revolution is an arguer. Sometimes we, the older generation, do not want to be contradicted, we want things to be set and we do not practice the typical revolutionary arguments. The revolution is an arguer, critical and thought-provoking. That is coming up in some youngsters: love for the revolution, even in a socialist country. There are ways to tell them that we are still living the revolution, giving them that happiness, there is no better way to be happy than in the revolution. Being a revolutionary is the nicest and hardest thing, it is the greatest duty, but there is no cheaper way to be happy.

Q: Has this been internalized by the Cuban Youth?

A: When the Socialist bloc fell, people thought that I changed and went to the right. I said, "this is marvelous," and they thought, "Celia is crazy." I always thought that the ideals of the October Revolution had been betrayed in the USSR, and when it fell I thought, "Cuba is stronger now, because this socialist revolution has not been betrayed, and Lenin is still well and alive over here, and we must take advantage of the life he still has. We have to pinch him, stimulate his energy, telling him that there is a big group of Cubans, Latin Americans, and people all over the world, who are still with him. If we have the courage to give that flag to our youth, they will fall in love with it. This is growing, and it is shown by the Five Heroes, not in a leaflet, but in real life. We must face the risks of being bold, because youth is bold, the revolution is there. A few days ago I was asked over here about critical thought, how it is being manifested in Cuba...

Q: And what did you answer?

A: There are channels in the Party and in the State, but all those things are done in reality, by men. The Party is not something abstract, it is formed by many comrades. Sometimes some people think that politics must be left for someone else, that it is better to go and have a beer. But it is not like that. Politics must be practiced with criticism, the struggle must be constant. Fidel is the first one about that. When there are criticisms about the revolution - we have the example of what happened with the power cuts now - Fidel is impressive: in those situations he goes and speaks directly with the people, in a direct dialogue. But we know that not everything can be resolved that way. The way to do it is to struggle for ideas to manifest themselves.

Q: What is the effect of the economic changes on Cubans?

A: At the Cuban Communist Party we still have a lot to learn, we must struggle to understand youth's new realities. Lenin lived through something similar in relation to the NEP, with joint ventures, although Cuba has most of the stocks and has the power to close the corporations whenever it wants.

Of course, those related to these corporations live reality in a set way. It is funny, but although the money is not for them, the dynamic when working as a director of a joint venture or a business changes your mentality, it changes you into a globalized being. Cuba is not exempt from this new phenomenon. Our challenge is telling them that there is another life, much more fun, more committed, something to give your life for.

There are many communists thinking like me. This is a good time. Fidel knows very well what to target. And youth must fill those spaces where we, those with white hair, are. That space is theirs, belongs to them. Proletariat internationalism is an interesting subject, and people should not relate to that only because of solidarity or good will. Internationalism is not that, it is the center of the revolution.

I am in Cuba because we must struggle in Cuba, but I am going to be the same way in Argentina, Scotland or the U.S. The advantage of socialist ideas is that they are international, compared to any other important social movement, which are always geographically grouped. "Proletariats of the world, unite," is a watchword without competition. A broadly humanist idea. The most humanist of them all. Communism is the only way humanity can be happy.

Q: The right wing is always talking about "the transition without Fidel."

A: And I ask them, what happened when Che died? Che is over there, as alive as always, he came back before Christ did. If Fidel dies, the world will lose a person whom perhaps they did not know how to make good use of as they should have. But there is a lot to be done yet, and the enemy is so ignorant and so clumsy that they do not realize that Fidel will hurt them much more when he's not around, because he is going to grow. The small criticisms he has now, which he gets as a statesman, will disappear, and only the immensity of a man will remain.

Communist ideas transcend Fidel Castro, as they transcended Lenin. The Revolution is endless in Cuba, and we are prepared for that. They asked me in Barcelona, in the International Conference, whether Socialism is possible in just one country. Socialism in one country does not work. It did not work in the USSR, but, what is critical is that neither Socialism nor the country remained. Socialism is international. Socialist revolutions exist, they work, and I am proud to having grown up in one of them.

The most authentic revolution in the West is in Cuba, no doubt about it, and now, of course, Chavez's, which must continue on the way to radicalization, and from there, as Che said, "many Vietnams", that is the solution for Latin America and the world. That is the attitude, permanent revolution, the revolution in Latin America intended by Che Guevara.

Published by Nuestra Propuesta, December, 2004.

NOTE

[1] This is a reference to the apartment where Abel made his revolutionary plans. It is on Calle 25 near Radio Havana Cuba.

"They are all the same."

In 1952, Raúl Gómez García, Jesús Montané and Abel Santamaría, three future Moncadistas, started the underground newspaper "Son los mismos" ("They are all the same.") They would cleverly say that everybody in the enemy camp belonged to the same group: the tyranny, the authentic politicians, even those from the Orthodox Party. The two last ones, due to their blindness or lack of loyalty. In the end, all of them are useless for the country. I always wondered who the other ones were. Those opposed to these ones. Ever since then, I use these words when I want to simplify about those who are not with the Man, for whatever reason. They are all the same....

San Jose, Costa Rica, lost many attendees who had been invited to the dance.... Only half of the invited presidents attended the XIV Ibero-American Summit. Just because the Pacific Rim Forum was taking place in Chile. It was supposed to be more important, because the attendee countries were richer. I mean richer, because their economic development was greater.

It looks as if the recently re-elected President of the United States, and suggestive China, were much more eye-catching than the weak American countries, especially in relation to education, which was the main topic of the San Jose Conference.

Although, really, the main topic of the 1995 Bariloche Conference was education. There are millions of 10-year-olds, who, ever since, do not know how to count nor how to write a single letter. Neither San Jose, nor Bariloche, will do anything for education. We will go back to discuss education ten years from now; at that time the children that were born during the Bariloche Summit (if they were able to survive), will in turn have illiterate children. So many broken agreements and such indolence about humanity are really disconcerting. My uncle Abel would say: "They are all the same…"

The news arrived, however, at that time, that Canada, Cuba, Finland and South Korea had received a recognition from UNESCO as a High

Performance Group, the highest educational recognition in the world. The experiences of these four countries in the field of education should be a guideline around the world, which in the last analysis is the *raison d'etre* of the recent Summit. UNESCO's officials should ask these countries how they have been able to achieve these miracles. I don't think that there is a more urgent miracle than education. That's the only way we will be able to avoid being prey to the epidemic of stupidity which has colonized the XXI Century.

The United States and China, in spite of their rapid economic development, are not included in that list; we must ask the reason. Venezuela, on the other hand, in recent years has had an unprecedented education campaign, using thousands of new experiences, including those from Cuba. Therefore, the most interesting aspect of the Summit would have been the visit of the President of Venezuela. Venezuela is not part of those four countries, but it will be. It is the country with the highest educational growth in the world.

A couple of days before, some Cuban "dissidents" decided to fix the San Jose celebration. It seems that terrorist Carlos Alberto Montaner and his collaborators did not learn about the UN news on education, and took part in an action supporting Cuban "democracy." Genius! The truth is found in the relation between the two events: on the one hand Cuba receives a recognition from the UN because of its educational achievements, on the other, the Cuban Revolution is at fault because it does not defend democracy. If two plus two still are four, then we must admit that in Cuba there are many dictators, who make women give birth to live children, and, under terror, they force those children to learn to read, at an age in which most children in the world enjoy human rights such as child prostitution, illiteracy, and death.

In San Jose, Costa Ricans defended the morality of the Americas, and did not allow in Costa Rica the farce which took place in Prague. With hand made signs and tightly closed fists, they defeated this project of tens of millions of dollars and prevented the meeting where the farce of helping democracy in Cuba was going to be implemented. On the other hand, the Chilean people put on their best show for the Forum of the Pacific Rim. After all, these summits are useful. They unite our peoples in the streets and invite us to the struggle. That will be the major contribution to these presidents' meetings.

Fidel could not attend the Ibero American Summit. He was injured just because he was working on education, during the graduation ceremonies of no less than four thousands art teachers. Chavez could not either, because a few hours before, Attorney General Danilo Anderson had been murdered, with a cowardly explosive in his car.

"Danilo was a man who symbolized the Bolivarian process. In the corrupt, classist, Venezuelan justice system, he was one of the few attorneys who applied the law to the pro-coup and criminal individuals associated with national subversion, who had to challenge their impunity. (...) Danilo presented a double threat to Washington's terrorist plans: he was taking one of its main power tools, the corrupt justice system of the Venezuelan upper class, and was becoming a symbol of the honest and useful patriot for the majority of the new Bolivarian Fatherland."

They are not doing anything new. Tens of years trying to oust the Cuban Revolution have not offered the enemy any new variants in their "struggle." A few months ago they murdered an engineer from PDVSA. We could trace almost a perfect parallel between the methods used in both cases. The assassination attempts against Commander Fidel Castro, the murder of our teachers, the explosions of La Coubre ship and a Cuban plane, etc.... Nothing has changed. And, why? Because they are all the same, they have always been all the same, because they do not even have the scruples to look for another peninsula in the United States besides Florida, nest of cowards, traitors and assassins, who dressed up in tuxedos, encourage a pathetic conference on democracy, and at the same time do not hesitate to assassinate a prosecutor... We already should be used to that.

They are undoubtedly supported by the CIA, and the U.S. Government tolerates them. Three of the criminals who were acquitted by the Ex-President of Panama, are now showing off somewhere else. The ex-President, in turn, certainly needed the money from her people to pay for dresses and jewellery. She had the gall to make a public announcement about it. She is shameless. I still cannot understand how in the San Jose summit a resolution against terrorism is launched, if one of those four assassins is surely hiding in a Central American country.

They cannot hide, the dirty water has already been served on the table. The tolerance and impunity offered by the recently re-elected President of the United States, accomplice of Anderson's assassination and other murders which must still be investigated. Because all the purged Cabinet of the Empire has left to do, is to put their white hoods on, upholding their racial superiority. And the cameras will be able to show the Secretary of State with blue eyes. They have got the American people used to so many lies, that Ms. Condoleezza Rice could easily obtain a pure Anglo Saxon past.

This fundamentalist and ignorant clique will continue protecting the criminals making attempts against the young Venezuelan Revolution. In the end, they are protecting the assassins of Prosecutor Anderson. It is sad, but in this history, anyone who is truly united is the enemy: the pathetic Conference in Prague and in San Jose for democracy in my country, the death of Prosecutor Anderson, and those responsible for the extermination in Fallujah.... are all the same. They have the same motivations and obey the same interests.

We must still hear Bush in Santiago de Chile, "scolding" Iran and North Korea because they are not "behaving right." Terrorism. It is laughable. There are many of us who are still ensnared in the enemy's verbal trap. Terrorism, axis of evil, struggle for freedom and all that phantasmagoric verbiage of the White House. Without realizing it, we follow them, and we complicate our discourse with so much phraseology.

There is something which could save us, Newton's Third Law of Motion.

Newton worked in our favor. The Third Law of Motion states, "Every action is followed by an equal and opposite reaction."

They are all the same, and that implies that we must also be all the same, against them.

Yes, Anderson's murder is another idiocy of the enemy who is running around, blind, deaf and dumb. The rule is as follows: for every crime they commit, more revolution for us. Yes. Us. Anderson's murder will promote the radicalization of the revolutionary process in Venezuela.

And Venezuela follows Newton. In the campaign of October 31, when 20 of the 22 states joined the Bolivarian Revolution, Commander Chavez defined the radicalization in the Venezuelan process. Radical is not synonymous with extremist. Extremes never go anywhere. The word radical comes from "root."

And we mean the root of Venezuela's problems. The enemy is not only isolated, but it is dressed again in the assassin's garb. It triggers anger and hate, instead of fear. "God first blinds those he wants to destroy," the saying goes. In those elections Chavez not only launched the war against large estates but against bureaucracy. Chavez is not only planning against the ills of capitalism, but against the ills a different society may have. Bureaucracy. Corruption and Bureaucracy are two ills which must be stopped when there's still time.

In a recent "Alo Presidente" programme, Commander Chavez spoke a lot about Che. Fortunately Che is being liberated from that romantic and Quixotic aura put on him in many places. Jose Marti must be liberated from the same thing. Che is indispensable for us, not only as the heroic guerrilla fighter, but also as a founder of Socialism and a socialist thinker, who gave so much to revolutionary theory and praxis.

This month was the 45th anniversary of the first voluntary work promoted in Cuba by Che. Referring to the book "
The Road to Fire, by Orlando Borrego, Chavez talks about the "prolific work by Che" as a leader of the Cuban Revolution, and, more specifically, as Secretary of Industry, about his drive in "analyzing different problems stated in the Handbook of Political Economy by the Academy of Sciences of the Soviet Union," written at that time under Stalin's orders," about the key issue in the construction of Socialism. He was terribly mystified by the Soviet political economy, about the connections in the development of productive forces, changes in the relations between production and advances of socialist awareness.

Chavez continues, "Socialist economic theory states that the previous development of productive forces is necessary, so that later the relations of socialist productivity can develop (...) but Che says that in underdeveloped countries, Cuba, for example, it was impossible to wait a hundred years for the development of productive forces and then change productive relations, Che stated, and I agree with Che, it is possible to raise workers' awareness, developing an awareness which goes further than Capitalism. We are doing that over here, we cannot wait until industry develops and national productivity gains impetus, that is, for the development of forces behind productivity to the extent that the development will affect productive relations and [generate] a new economic model."

There are many who still doubt the Venezuelan President, with infantile allegations, or interpret his actions entrenched in textbook paradigms. I said it before, and it is not a metaphor, that the triumph of August 15 has the same importance as November 7 or January 1. We, Communists, could have the same experience as in Cuba. When the Communist Party started taking seriously the movement of July 26 and Fidel Castro, Fidel and the Cuban Revolutionaries were already far ahead in the race.

Fidel said in March, 1956, "The July 26th Movement is the revolutionary organization of the poor, for the poor and by the poor. The July 26th Movement is the hope of redemption for the Cuban working class..." Those who suspected that the July 26th Movement was a proletarian revolutionary organization were just a few. Imperialism, and almost all the "traditional" communist parties did not realize, until the end, who Fidel was. We can fall into the same trap with Hugo Chavez.

Hugo Chavez is going after two things: the revolution within the revolution, war against bureaucracy, and the need for the integration of the Americas. We can say it in a different way: permanent revolution and internationalism. Commander Chavez is saying that he is not an ex-rebel, but a rebel. Anyone who has been a true rebel never stops being a rebel. Fidel has just loudly stated that "On facing yesterday's deadly perils and today's, which are still worse, Socialism will definitely be the only real hope for peace and the survival of our species." Always the same rebel... the same communist, different from so many intellectuals who think the word socialism is useless in their discourse.

Because, as Bertolt Brecht said, the good men struggle for a day. "But there are those who struggle their whole lives, and they are indispensable." Together with them, we will all be able "to change this Earth, once and for all."
November, 2004.

Fidel and Chávez together and in red... this November 7

On November 7, I like to visit Lenin Hill in Regla. Regla is a little seaside town in Havana that is reached by crossing the bay. The Virgen de Regla is the patron of the city. Consequently, when we arrive she receives us flirtatiously, with her blue dress ... announcing the certain victory of the Industriales, her baseball team in the coming championships.

Lenin is higher up. In 1924, a communist mayor decided to build the monument as a beautiful Cuban tribute to the leader of the workers. I think that it is the first one dedicated to Lenin outside the USSR . I insist that Cuban nationality is adorned by brush strokes of love that foster a new internationalism. Blessed be my compatriots of Regla! These days, mostly after November 2, Lenin and the Black Virgin must have chatted quite a bit. She, fearful for the fate of the Cubans and the poor of the world. He, concerned to see if we communists are capable of overcoming the last blows of the enemy.

The flowers for November 7 are bought in front of the church. The beautiful Virgin always offers the freshest ones to her comrade up on the Hill. Let no one mistakenly think that the interests of this compañera lie in the pitiful phrases from Rome nor those of a Pole holding up a cross ... that certainly has nothing to do with the spirit of that Palestine which died at the hands of the Zionists for defending the poor of the Land. No, the Caribbean Virgin, undoubtedly, blesses these hundreds of children who should be able to live every year in their country and those elderly people who should not die of hunger.

The port can be seen from the Hill. For more than ten years those, who called themselves heirs of the man of the Hill, decided, with a brush stroke, not to help Cuba or the Virgen de Regla, or the children, or the elderly. In the name of freedom, they decided to put us in the hands of imperialism. They failed in their purpose. My country not only saved itself from all this, and with its virgins, but Cuba saved the honor of the October revolution. During those hard years, the words "Socialism or Death" found those Europeans who sought refuge in this little island.

That is why, today, the best communist celebration took place. No! It had nothing to do the words of His Excellency, the Russian Ambassador to Cuba . This man cannot know how to talk of the October Revolution. Rather he could talk of the history of the Czars and the Orthodox Church, never of the Bolshevik revolution, nor of the flag of the proletariat. They lowered the red flag in that embassy. I think there is no celebration without that color. If there is a flag that lowered the flag of the communists from many places on a November 7 … it is the flag of the Russian Republic . To tell the truth, in all parts except Coyoacán where Leon Trotsky guards it.

The anniversary of the October Revolution was celebrated in Havana … in the Council of State and Ministers: On the 6th, in the evening, Comandante Chávez decided to visit his injured colleague. During those eight hours of the visit, in a warm embrace, the world revolution fused for a second. At that moment, under the silent notes of the International, Lenin again raised his voice to the workers and the red army again shook the world. Its legendary head was also included in that embrace, although he was 126 years old. The red flag of Coyoacán unfurled its wings seeing the two best revolutionaries of the world. In that embrace, there was the first little piece of hope. That hope that seemed to disappear this past November 2 …

This is what happened: Hugo Chávez appeared at the door of the office, fresh as the sea, with a light colored shirt and sneakers. This color highlighted the intense bronze of his skin in complicity with his wide smile and eyes that revealed an original beauty. He made his greeting with the right hand in a frank military salute. He walked slowly over, smilingly and moving his head from side to side, in a familiar gesture. The open smile that turned into open laughter. Fidel was there. Fidel was seated. He had seriously injured his knee and right arm on October 20. Fidel greeted his comrade with the left hand, with his favorite hand! Chavez approached, bent down and with both hands on the shoulder of the legendary guerrilla repeated a familiar phrase "You're all right Fidel, all right" And yes he was! Even with his leg stretched out and his right arm in a sling, he was overwhelmingly happy. But, how strange was Fidel? For a moment, I didn't understand. Fidel wasn't dressed in his military greens. Fidel was … in red. A deep red that projects optimism to the very stars seeing their young comrade. In red. Why was he in red?

It is the color of the Bolivarian revolution that had won a popular victory on October 31. Coincidentally it is the color of the world revolution, the color of the October Revolution. Fidel was expressing to Chavez, with that color that he, together with all of us, had participated in the elections of October 31 where we were victorious.

These elections were, undoubtedly, a deepening of the ones of August 15. Chávez made no shady deals, he deceived no one, did not have to resort to personal gossip about his adversaries, he did not have to invest hundreds of millions of dollars. His campaign, colored in red and sincerity, appealed to the truth. That truth that endows the best revolutionary of Venezuela to be the legitimate president. He resorted to his allies of the past. Che whom he considers an "infinite and immortal revolutionary". The revolution in Venezuela is willing to "be real", as Che said in his farewell letter to Fidel. Therefore, in the Bolivarian revolution "we conquer or we die". In his victory campaign Chávez did not talk of what Venezuela had achieved, he spoke of what had to be done. "The deep problem of Venezuela is the exclusion and poverty and even more, the dire poverty". He unleashed a battle with no quarter given to bureaucracy and against the large land holdings. He asked each elected Chavista governor "to become (...) the head of the struggle against the large land holdings".

"Now Venezuela is entering a new stage, the Bolivarian revolution must be deepened, it must be more a revolution every day, more authentic, truer, the structural transformation of the economy, society is the grand challenge we face now", Chavez says. "Poverty, misery, exclusion will not be solved with lukewarm cloths. Simon Bolivar said clearly "The political gangrenes are not cured with palliatives; I could add: the political gangrenes are not cured with palliatives. The only way, the true way, we must accept it thus, understand it thus: each day more of us could lead our country in the full social and economic revolution that is through a full revolution, an integral revolution, a revolution that must work at the economic level; in other words a revolution should be, in addition to political, social, economic in depth. I will say it now, we must leave behind the capitalist model that ruled in Venezuela for so long; within a framework of the capitalist model, the economic capitalist model is not the solution to the serious problems of society, of poverty, of misery, of exclusion".

Che would have said it with fewer words: "Socialist revolutions or caricatures of revolution".

Perhaps this revolutionary does not know that José Martí said in his radical speech 'Insufficient politics': "Remedies are important when the relationship of the diseases are not analyzed with strength and urgency. (…) Politics is a guilty occupation when they hide from it (…) the deep poverty and dire misfortune, the dire poverty and misfortune of the people". The policies of Chavez are more than enough. "Homeland or death" is the slogan of the Venezuelan commandant. But José Martí said "Homeland is Humanity". In Cuba , another necessary word was added to make it true: Socialism. This slogan that, taken to its utmost consequences, is the slogan of the world.

I've been wondering how two peoples with barely two days' difference between them can choose such opposites. The US people subscribed to war; the Venezuelan to revolution.

Nothing much can be gathered from television and, however, two men were observed who, in spite of a cool November, it was very clear on camera. Chavez bowed to greet him and ratify his commitment. Fidel proudly pointed to the two small flags of the two countries embroidered in his pocket.

They spent eight hours together. I don't know what they talked about but as you and I can imagine they talked of: the great victory of October 31; the victory of the Frente Amplio whose true victory must now be observed with concrete actions; the recent Rio Summit; where, in fact, President Chávez announced a "strange" observation for those planning to fight poverty and hunger in the south of my continent. His words were, more or less: "I don't know how it can be done through a capitalist economy". And, above all else, they must have talked of the triumph of reaction in the United States . A good agenda for a November 7.

At the end, in front of the TV cameras, Chavez dons a beautiful shirt… a red one his comrade had given him, after receiving a painting of Bolivar by Valdés, an artist of the westernmost province of the Island.

It is now November 7 and Chávez will have to leave but not forgetting with that small acute look that Fidel and he were "sharing their souls" as a journalist commented.

I looked at Fidel again. I thought of those years of infinite struggle swimming against the current. It still goes on and his wounds are from combat. It wasn't an accident at home working in the garden, as with many men of his age, but winning more battles of ideas.

José Martí said: "When there are many men without honor, there are always men who have the honor of many men. Those are the ones who rebel with a terrible force against those who steal freedom from the people that is to steal honor from men. In these men there are thousands of men, an entire people, human dignity."

And at this point in time, on November 7 of this year, human dignity multiplied in this meeting of love.

Then I did not suffer much for not having visited Lenin in Regla. These two men in red gave me the perfect celebration and my November 7 renewed my desire to fight. The first battle we will wage will be to morally teach the US people that they are being bewitched by an evil of so many years.

We will fight with all our strength, happy, knowing that the red flag now flutters over a new peoples of South American in a permanent revolution. And that color will extend throughout the continent and leap across the Atlantic and reach the beautiful Europe where we have so many comrades who are red inside and go down to Africa and reach the poles. And the Land will again turn in the right direction in relation to the sun...

I recalled with warmth and relevance Trotsky's slogan: dum spiro spero (while there is a murmur of life there is hope).

And still, I am asked in many places ... what will happen when Fidel goes...Fidel will not go for me. I believe that Chávez is only about 50. *November, 2004.*

November 2: Diagnosis Confirmed

For Carl Sagan

Nothing that happens in the world these days can be compared to what occurred on Election Day in the United States of America.

I'm not referring to the implications for Cuba over the next four years. They won't change much. After more than 40 years replete with hate and hostility, the Cuban Revolution has, paradoxically, the best weapons with which to face the coming four years and, even if the US continues with the same, the next four millennia ...

Thanks to privation, organization and courage, my people are vaccinated against the Empire.

They say that "our brave dissidents" were in the US Interests Section in Havana where they followed the US elections and where naturally Bush was elected with more than 80% (not sure where her figure comes from here). With their lack of culture and their servility, they don't stop offering us reasons to hold them in contempt.

I will neither talk about the misfortune that this re-election bodes for the Middle East because it is unfortunate enough to possess oil. I am not even going to talk about the 100,000 people murdered in an incomprehensible war, where they haven't captured the bad guy, nor has the good guy won. Simple mathematics tells us how many more are condemned to die.

In writing these lines, I will also try not to think of the horrors the children of Palestine suffer, where an almost infantile unconditional support is granted to Sharon and his Nazi intentions.

Nor do I address "Our Americas", which will have to continue fighting tooth and nail against the White House agenda that either the presidents of our countries vote against or quite seriously face extermination through whatever new idiocy that emanates from it.

A sad and naive conceit exists among the people of the United States who are the first victims of these long years of spiritual corruption by their government. Yes, the people of the United States. They chose the world's Emperor.

Back in Rome the slaves did not vote - we are those slaves. The small difference in this comparison is that "the free people" in those times had more culture than today's "free people". At least they listened to their philosophers and thinkers. Brutus went to extremes in his assassination of Julius Caesar, but for good or bad the problems of state were taken with greater seriousness.

Like it or not, the people who filled the streets of the United States to vote took in their hands the small hope of humanity that aspires to that euphemism of a better world that they say is possible. The people of the USA should have voted for the tens of thousands of men who are going to die in the wars, for the tens of thousands of children who in these last four years have not reached an age to say "mother". They should have voted to protect the sea and the sky, and not infest our common home with every type of weapon. They should have voted to prevent the waste of public funds on bombers and their intelligent bombs so we could invest more in the sciences. We could discover a cure for cancer, a vaccine for AIDS or at least reduce the cost of its treatment. With such resources, the people of the USA could have given us the thrill of seeing with our own eyes the beginning of the Universe through the Superconducting Supercollider project. We would thus see all the laws that drive the Universe that fused and were created in one great explosion. Poets, philosophers and politicians would fall to their knees embracing each other in ratifying this miracle, this extraordinary effort of creation that we are destroying.

These people took to the ballot boxes the hopes of billions of people, of ants, of electrons and stars that aspire not to be destroyed.

But we do not have the right to demand something of them for which they are not prepared - for they are victims more than we.

I ask for a moment of compassion for the people of the United States.

It's not that I think that the alternative was better. Not at all. The Democratic Party campaign was the same, but used "other methods". Kerry had the gall to say that he would have attacked Iraq knowing that it did not have weapons of mass destruction. But the NO to Bush was a good symptom of recovery.

Far better to have abstained. But no, Bush obtained a greater number of votes than any other president since 1988. We might think that there are millions of people that are in effect accomplices to the horrors lived these last four years. But no, they are not the perpetrators of these acts.

They are like us: they have two arms, they love their children, they cry for their dead like the rest of humanity.

Why then, faced with the evidence, faced with a brave and charismatic man like Michael Moore who gathered an impressive audience with his movie Fahrenheit 9/11, did they not jump, intrigued, at the possibility of discovering the truth? Why they did not see, as we saw them, the frightful photos of the prisoners in the naval base at Guantánamo or at Abu Ghraib?

Why did they not demand to see the weapons of mass destruction that justified the war? Those weapons that, with total disregard for the intelligence of the US populace, Bush tried to find in his drawer, where he no doubt hides his little lead soldiers and his clay cowboys. Do they not know of the Palestinian girl riddled with 25 bullets by a Zionist? And Enron? And September 11? How can a people trust a government which allowed a few fanatics to hijack scheduled airliners underneath their noses and destroy the emblematic World Trade Center?

Do they need glasses, or the Internet, or television sets? No, unfortunate people: they need culture, the ability to reason and the need to cure themselves of their chronic hedonism.

Of course, if I really believed that President George W. Bush speaks with God, I would vote for him too. It would be interesting to ask him in which language they spoke: Aramaic, Hebrew or Latin? It would also be good to know if he spoke with the son of God, that son of Palestine who died at the hands of the Jews, or only spoke with the God of the Torah?

Take for example the subject of abortion, which was one of the main issues in this election. The right or not to interrupt a pregnancy. This brings us to the true tragedies of this planet:

What do they defend? Life, no doubt.

Carl Sagan says "Today, no right to life exists in any society ...

Animals are raised on farms for sacrifice, forests destroyed, rivers and lakes contaminated until no fish can live in them. We kill red deer and elk for sport ... every day we cause the extinction of a species. All these beasts and plants are as alive as we are."

Ah, you say, but were we not talking about human life?

Sagan continues: "There's no protection for the tens of thousands of children under five that perish every day on this planet because of preventable reasons such as starvation, dehydration, diseases, and negligence."

The November 2nd voters who worried so much about abortion, did not spare the time to consider the "collateral damage" that their leaders murder using their taxes. But these children do not deserve to be called human beings: they come into this world with the sole object of rendering service to US weaponry.

The people of the US have been robbed of the possibility of deciding their own interests. They have been made sick. In my opinion, the first wound to heal should be the wounded soul of the people of the USA. I think we have been selfish. Our children die of hunger, fall beneath bombs, but US babies are abducted at birth - and not by extraterrestrials. Or, perhaps, yes. These terrible leaders should be expunged from the Earth as they neither respect nor feel bound by the most basic elements of life. Their children grow up without understanding the responsibility of being a citizen of the country that runs the world. People in the US die without any concern other than that they were unable to change their car from the previous year's model.

It wasn't always this way: "From the glorious days of the most vehement freedom was born the United States", says José Martí, who, perhaps, loved the country more than any other.

The United States had scientists as its leaders - Jefferson was one. At what point in time did this generous nation turn around its refinement of the sciences, the arts and its love of liberty?

I don't know, and the fault shouldn't only lie with them. For some strange internal reason I also hold that other power responsible in whose hands the world was once balanced. The world entered into complete darkness when the USSR and the USA agreed enthusiastically on peaceful coexistence. They sickened and contaminated us with disease from one end (of the planet) to the other. Feudal dogmatism disguised as socialism with a growing market mentality and domination now runs the Earth. They are not opposite poles. No! Enough! They are two monsters with hidden bridges of collaboration. This was evident in the (1962) Missile Crisis. We are all equally guilty.

Carl Sagan was one of my prophets. He dedicated his life and his intelligence to teach his people the responsibility of being from the USA and how to be inhabitants of the Earth. His films and his books are so marvelous they fill our eyes with tears. His science classes were poetry. My growing debt to Nature is thanks to this man. When I go to the market it is he that prevents me from taking another plastic bag that takes Nature thousands of years to biologically disintegrate.

At one point the USSR and the USA spoke of joining forces against an alien invader. Sagan said in his book *Thousands of Millions* that "we are in danger, and not from alien invaders...We have generated sufficient risks on our own...Our common enemies are more tiring and difficult to hate ... The joining of forces against these new adversaries force us to come to the self-realization that we ourselves are responsible for what we are facing today".

Carl Sagan was not a communist and loved the United States as much as the best of its citizens. He was proud of the founding fathers of his country: "Jefferson was one of my first heroes, not for his scientific interests (although they helped him to mould his political philosophy) but for the fact that he more than almost anyone else was responsible for extending democracy to the world. The idea…is that neither kings, nor priests, nor the mayors of great cities, nor dictators, nor military cliques, nor conspiracies of rich people, but rather the ordinary people working together should govern nations".

And now less than 10 years after Sagan's death, who governs the country of Thomas Jefferson and Carl Sagan? What have they done with the ordinary people of the USA? Why is it that not only was there a record turn-out, not only did the Republicans win more seats in the Senate and four religious extremists win in the South, but that Bush also won the popular vote? This government has the vote of the majority of people in the USA.

In a way, Carl Sagan foresaw this. In all his books, in all his sentences, in every word, he insists on the need for skepticism. For a long time the people of the US have been robbed of their willpower. They vote for hair dyes or mixer brands or much worse. They're convinced they're undergoing a nuclear threat. Their job is to consume French fries and drink Coca Cola and watch horror movies or football games.

Their leaders will take care of the Universe for them. They only have to pay some tax and vote every four years. The rest of the world doesn't exist. Iraq and Afghanistan don't exist. The 100,000 dead are a lie. Spiderman, Batman and Superman will protect them. Disappearing Africa is a lie. Extraterrestrial terrorists in their flying saucers are planning nuclear war against America and so they need a president who can handle that.

Scientific illiteracy, said Sagan in *The World and its Demons,* extends to 98% of the US population. These are the ones who will decide our future.

According to James Petras "Bush is a fundamentalist Christian who, rejecting the scientific community, proclaims the biblical history of creationism denigrating the known scientific basis of evolution that is taught in high schools and universities".

But George W Bush is not just any president. He's the president of the most powerful nation ever, keeper of the most advanced technologies, world dictator of how we must behave. He probably spends huge amounts of his free (free?) time playing Nintendo, so who is civilizing whom? Who is really civilized?

We will never know, as Sagan said, to what level ignorance contributed to the decline of ancient Athens, but the consequences of scientific illiteracy are far more dangerous in our time than any time before. Humanity is too close to the products of science, but too far from them to understand their transcendental nature, their dangers or benefits.

Sagan predicted what is happening in the United States. He said that (only) the scientific mind, the ability to reason and to question would save the essence of his country.

"In a way people have lost the ability to form priorities, clutching onto magic crystals or pyramids and nervously consulting horoscopes, unable to discern between what makes them feel good and what is real, and without realizing it, we continue to slide into superstition and obscurity."

Thus the popular president of the United States uses his faculties to declare, within two days of his reelection, the privatization of social security, tax code reform, and the intensification of the war on Iraq.

Michael Moore follows in the footsteps of Carl Sagan. Like many intellectuals and artists he took his camera and his money to the voting booth, preferring not to win a prize to see if he was able to convince. He tried to show his country what he thought.

And he called on the same means, for *Fahrenheit 9/11* is a scientific documentary - concrete and didactic. He asks questions and outlines open answers.

I don't know is Moore has ever read Karl Marx, but he ends his documentary saying that "the foundation of high society can only (be built) on the foundation of poverty and ignorance".

There it is: poverty is us and the rest of the world - poor and helpless...I worry about the ignorance of the citizens of the United States of America who in some way on November 2nd chose a government that does not have the capacity to look after us, nor (indeed) them.

I don't want to be a pessimist, which is why we should urgently propose that Moore work with us and all the others who think the same way. The people of the United States were responsible for ending the Vietnam War in that miracle that took place in the 1960s. We need to once more win over its talented journalists, politicos, artists, scientists and workers. Get them to listen once more to the words of John Lennon's *Imagine* or get them to show *The Great Dictator* on a giant screen in the ruins of the Trade Centre, or use Walt Whitman in an urgent battle to pool the minds

of these brothers and sisters that on November 2nd confirmed that they were pulled in like fish with bait and tackle, and that they are today the depositories of the biggest farce that has ever been imposed on any people in history.
November, 2004.

Cuba, Venezuela, and Latin America: Is the revolutionary flame spreading?

Q: As a Cuban communist, how do you see the revolutionary process in Venezuela?

The Bolivarian revolution finds much support not only from the communists of many years and experience but also among the young people for whom the live revolutionary process of Venezuela awakens more enthusiasm than boring and monotonous rhetoric of "socialism". Once, Che Guevara spoke of making "many Vietnams" in Latin America. Now we face this task again and have the possibility of deepening the Bolivarian revolution and consolidating it as a socialist revolution. The impulse for socialist revolution in all of Latin America can and should come from Venezuela. The idea of a permanent revolution that Che also fought for is relevant today.

A: But some fear that a socialist revolution in Venezuela could provoke the reactionaries and even the unleashing of a military invasion. Do you think that Hugo Chavez has been "intelligent" in the past few weeks seeking a form of consensus in negotiations with business organization?

Reaction knows what it wants and does not need to be provoked. I expect that Hugo Chavez will not fall into a reformist trap and make concessions to his sworn enemies. The Venezuelan oligarchy needs to win time. When conditions are right, the oligarchy will try to eliminate Chavez in the same manner that the Chilean ruling class eliminated their socialist president, Salvador Allende, and with him many left wing activists in 1973. The majority of the Venezuelans, undoubtedly, would fight against an invasion as the Cubans did in the Bay of Pigs in 1961. Under these circumstances, as internationalists, we must help the Venezuelan revolution as the international brigades did in the Spanish civil war in 1936.

Q: But the Cuban Revolution. Hasn't it survived for 45 years without having to "export" its revolution?

A: Revolutionary Cuba has persisted due to the decisive break of Fidel Castro with capitalism and imperialism. Through my experiences in the German Democratic Republic and Cuba, I have reached the conclusion that "socialism in only one country" is impossible. The extension of the revolution throughout the Latin American continent is essential for the survival of the Cuban revolution.

Venezuelan oil at low prices alleviates the energy crisis of Cuba and the Cuba doctors and teachers help the poor in Venezuela to develop their own honor and self esteem. These special relations that exist between Cuba and revolutionary Venezuela give us a glimpse of the enormous possibility and the progress that could come about with a network of democratically planned economies throughout Latin America, free of imperialistic paternalist interference. In the end, an isolated revolutionary Cuba could not survive.

Q: Do you think that Cuba will end up like the GDR and suffer a capitalist counter-revolution?

A: I think that there is a real danger that this could happen and every honest revolutionary that I know has the same fear. Although the planned economy in Cuba is monopolized by foreign trade, although the means of production are the property of the state and the majority of joint ventures are controlled by the state, our time is running out. Dollarization has already had negative effects. The heads of the joint ventures and those responsible for foreign trade are at risk of being bought out and could be susceptible to bourgeois ideas. If the exiled Cuban capitalists return and try to take over the country with the help of pro-capitalist and pro-imperialist forces we would face a threat of counter-revolution and the worst kind of capitalism. All the achievements of the past 45 years are in danger. That is why we must defend the revolutionary legacy of Lenin, Trotsky and Che Guevara and move forward the global revolution.

Interview with Hans-Gerd Öfinger, September, 2004.

The magnetism of
the Permanent Revolution

The island of the Renaissance man, Thomas Moore, is unattainable. Luckily we live in a world that will always be perfectible and that humans are the most nonconformist under the rays of the sun. But a utopia will continue to be indispensable to modify reality and will continue to be the driving force of justice. According to José Ingenieros it is a mysterious expediency. It is also a sacred ember and if you lose this expediency you become a pure human trash. Above all, humanity needs to create systems of expediency that approximately point to the same direction to reach a good port.

The best and simplest simile I can find is magnetism: In ferromagnetic materials, a special for of interaction occurs between the adjacent atoms called: attraction by exchange. Applying an external magnetic field, the atoms are magnetized in the direction of that field. Removing this external charge, the system remains magnetized with a permanent ferromagnetism (the permanent magnets, for example). Now, if the temperature rises above a certain value, called Curie temperature, the interaction disappears. Ferromagnetism is an "ordered" state. Entropy reduces. The main parameters are: applied magnetic field, the magnetization that the system attains and the temperature that induces disorder in the system.

In society we must find a sufficiently large field to couple our "atoms" and have a permanent magnetism achieving a collective and international event, just like the atoms of the reduced world of the magnet, struggling always against the temperature that disrupts the order. It's simple: But, also, not all the elements of the periodic chart are orderly, regardless of the field you apply or by lowering the temperature. There are paramagnetism and diamagnetism, etc. Atoms that are not found ferromagnetism but line up with the field and when removed from the field they become disorderly or there are those that never orient themselves. Don't lose time with them, because you will never obtain ferromagnetism. Our task is to count on those that can attain orientation, only with them. Orient ourselves and construct a permanent magnet.

This simile allows me to place the proletariat in the transition group of Iron (elements capable of lining up), assuming temperature to present natural differences, the many currents that separate us, our infinite nonsense, for example; magnetism is the revolution that will decidedly be permanent; and the external field that form, undoubtedly, the political parties that spark the class struggle.

And when we reach port? The port is in the stars. Someone said once that triumphs are only an excuse to oil the rifles and continue forward. Che did not say it. But he did it ...

To what extent is the revolution permanent? Is it perhaps an attack of that fighter that killed Stalinism in Coyoacan, as so many others)? Perhaps rhetorically to handicap the proletariat from taking power, as many believe? We have lived this farce for decades. The permanent revolution does not refer to a simultaneous revolution. In fact, he who headed the Red Army in 1917 was Leon Trotsky. The one who first predicted the October proletarian revolution was Leon Trotsky. The permanent revolution is the only viable form of making a socialist revolution on an international scale. And this is the only scale that promotes the development of the Socialism we need, much more than the lost island of Saint Tomas Moro.

There are three reasons that explain that the socialist revolution is permanent:

First: In underdeveloped countries the road to democracy necessarily goes first through a dictatorship of the proletariat and not the other way around as had been thought.

Second: Once in the power of society, it begins to transform for an indefinite period. The many revolutions such as the economic, scientific, educational, develop in such a manner that the socialist revolution *never* achieves equilibrium.

And ... third is the international character. That is to say that a socialist revolution does not end with the dictatorship of the proletariat and does not end at national borders. The concept of permanent revolution by which Leon Trotsky was so criticized was also a scientific discovery, like ferromagnetism and, above all, a manual for action. It seems that these words do not roll easily in the language or are too big for the heart. The theory of permanent revolution contains the Lenin school and most consequent Marxism.

My revolution, the Cuban revolution is an unprecedented beacon, perhaps even without knowing that Leon Trotsky has been rigorous with these precepts. From Martí, passing by Julio Antonio [Mella], El Che and Fidel Castro, Lenin is still alive in America! Our homeland today holds forth the banners of the permanent revolution in three points. The battle of ideas, where there is no end to our educational and cultural plans; the Baraguá oath where, in the midst of countless hardships, we decided to fight imperialism to the end and in the Bolivarian revolution where thousands of Cuban physicians, teachers, technicians are participating as a small part of that people. We are a classic example of the permanent revolution that is permanent in time and space. It is brilliantly led by Fidel Castro. Whether Leon Trotsky was read or not. It's unimportant.

And capitalism... what port did all those clowns offer of the end of history to make us stay in front of the TV like donkeys? The proposed the crudest materialism to build who know what. I don't believe that this sorry state, in which we are incapable of sustaining the air we breathe, is truly a serious proposition. I still don't understand how many more opportunities they are going to have to offer us to understand that the result of these conservatives is only absurd wars, terrorism and misery.

It will take a long time, assuredly, the necessary time to activate the external magnetic field and begin to wake from the dream that the crisis of the left condemned us (that bet downward or upward, but never leftward).

There is no middle road or conciliation. No, socialism is not inevitable. Our alternative is ... barbarity; in the words of Friedrich Engels and Rosa Luxemburg. And socialism, not that bumbling caricature that Stalinism designed. That it only lasted 70 years and capitalism is lasting hundreds? No, not at all. There are still no explanations on why it lasted so long. The comparison is not valid; imperialism and its economic actions did not make capitalism in only one country. From Columbus to Coca Cola they have known how life is won. Capitalism, until recently, was consistent with its depraved mission.

Socialism has been one of the broadest ideals in the world. In spite of its failures and its converts who go to talk in congresses about any convoluted term and not of revolution, of taking power, of proletariat. Those who have already become pure human trash, using an engineering term, use terms that are silently disappearing from our political dictionary. And all this is to prevent being "committed". To avoid being committed ... with whom?

I recently read a vital article by James Petras on Venezuela and the referendum. The revolutionary government of President Chavez only has to be faithful to the one social class who went to the ballots until dawn on that August 15.

Petras said:

"In truth, the referendum was mainly based on a clear class and race division. Union leaders who were not tied to the opposition noted that more than 85% of the working class and poor workers voted for the president while early reports of voting in the wealthy neighborhoods gave a lower percentage of 80%. A similar process of polarization by class and race was obvious in the extraordinary participation in the polls and in the percentage of poor Afro-Venezuelans who increasingly voted for Chavez (71% of the electorate voted, an unprecedented number). Undoubtedly the president's success, closely linked to the programs of social assistance and class identity, were the basis of the electoral behavior".

Then it is clear with whom we must be committed in Venezuela. I say "we" fully aware that it is absurd that the Chavez government is the only one responsible for what occurs in that country. We are all connected. What happens in Panama, Colombia, London, Australia is the responsibility of all revolutionaries of the world.

Internationalism is not a sentiment of goodness or merciful complacency. International is the only route of the parties to make the revolution last. And without the lasting revolution, let's make paper flags for Christmas but we will be unable to build socialism. In trying, we have tried too much.

I say more: The desires of the French revolution, the social justice of the left wing social-democracies and even the gospel will now only be defendable from positions of class struggle. The mysterious expediency the engineers talk about tightening when the mobilizing struggle is for a necessary objective. The utopia we need is that will let us stand up in history with a Project. And the only viable Project is the socialist revolution.

Our continent opens up a promising space. The words of the real possibility is a socialist confederation in this part of the world, as brilliantly explained by Comrade Zbigniew Marcin Kowalewski [1], in this event, explained that it is a reality and is the most beautiful reality we could wish. Far are the furies that scourged the Southern Cone with the dictatorships. Of course, tomorrow (sic - the date written is not the one printed - the anniversary is September 11) is another anniversary of the massacre in Santiago de Chile. President Allende fell like a hero under the claws of the most sanguinary terrorist that today is trying to defend himself and his millions. My Chilean brothers did not have the chance to make war on the White House for having planned the terrorist attack in their country. They had to swallow their dead, their disappeared, and the songs of hope. A few days ago, another accomplice of international terrorism was set free in the most shameful and cynical manner, an assassin of dozens of compatriots. The indecency of the bourgeoisie is ripping off any permissible costume. They suffer the lies, the egotism and irrational desire for money that walks the Earth in its blue image. They are all the same, Pinochet, Moscoso, the White House, the IMF, and the OAS. They do not even differ in the color of their hair. The enemy is uniting. Let us do so also! They have nothing to offer our peoples. If WE manage to free ourselves from the collapse of European socialism that was merely a perversion, we have the island of the utopia as an achievable dream. The struggle under Jacobin banners now sounds sweeter, more coherent and more possible.

We have enough experience, comrades, we are lacking unity. Stalin, during the Second World War comforted the Soviet comrades with the pathetic phrase of "little mother Russia" to unite them. We don't need that. Thanks to the Internet our struggle can be worldwide and united.

I would found the International Solidarity Brigade. Since we all need all of us like atoms of my material. I still don't know today who suffers most, if my children due to the economic blockade of the United States or the children of a worker of the Unites States with the pestilence of their aberrant video games and pseudo scientists.

Fidel said in 1961: "We will first see a victorious revolution in the United States than a counterrevolutionary victory in Cuba". That Fidel is the same one who, in the midst of hunger fully designed by imperialism and the Stalin heirs: Socialism or Death, a slogan that all communists in the world should take up.

Undoubtedly, but that revolution in the United States should be socialist. Michael Moore has just renounced his Oscar nomination for exhibiting his documentary, Fahrenheit 9/11 on US television. Who are the victims of terrorism, the Iraqis or the US citizens that now have 1000 dead?

"The sudden blows reveal the core of things", José Martí said. And that happened that September 11 of 2001. The events of New York are the same that occurred in Palestine or in Buenos Aires one December or Madrid, or Moscow or Chechnya. On any front the world overflows and they still sit us down to wait for translators of the truth.

José Martí was a class fighter. It is tiring to give order to the world with phrases that have been said and that ignore, with utter lack of consideration, the truth of events. To say that José Martí was a petty bourgeois democrat is the same as saying the sea exists to contain the salt of our Sunday pasta. Martí founded the party fundamentally for the workers, the most radical revolutionary party of the time and place. The teachings of the previous were not in vain. Revolution was his constant word, the independence of Cuba was a mere event to oppose the class enemy that he was the first to describe. To be a Cuba was a mere detail of birth. He ended his days fighting for equilibrium of the world. His error was to die too soon (It is an epidemic of the revolutionaries).

Mentioning Karl Marx in 1883, on the eve of his death he noted:

"Karl Marx is dead, because he took sides with the weak he deserves honor. But he, who points to the damage and yearns with a generous desire to remedy the situation but points to a soft remedy for the harm, does no good. It is horrific to throw men against others."

A simple cup of coffee would have been enough for these two geniuses to come to an agreement. Marx proposed exactly this: "the only remedy to harm" and José Martí did this: "Throw some men over others".

We communists really need to unite and not in halls or congresses only, but in mass marches, in the banging of pots and pans, in Iraq, in Palestine. The communists must carry the impulse of the people in each battle against the injustices of the enemy. One by one and all at the same time.

The political parties should act as an external magnetic field that orients the spins of the atom. Trotsky said

"Only on the basis of a study of political processes in the masses themselves, can we understand the rôle of parties and leaders, whom we least of all are inclined to ignore. They constitute not an independent, but nevertheless a very important, element in the process. Without a guiding organization, the energy of the masses would dissipate like steam not enclosed in a piston-box. But nevertheless what moves things is not the piston or the box, but the steam." [2]

And I say more: We need only one Communist Party in the World "With all and for the good of all" according to Martí. I hope I live to see it.

In spite of it all, our differences are minimal in relation to the truth that makes us different from the enemy. If we talked with our dead they would all point to the same road.

Let us plan the work with strength and optimism. We have the best weapons: They only have human waste: the stupid war, the lack of culture, the corruption and terrorism. We have the dream of the revolution. Forward comrades! Socialism or Death!

Paper given at the workshop "The utopia that we need" sponsored by the Bolivar Marti Faculty in Central Havana, in September, 2004.

NOTE

[1] Zbigniew Kowalewski was in 1980-81 a member of the regional leadership of Solidarnosç in Lodz. As a delegate to the First Congress of Soldarnosç, he took part in the elaboration of the programme that was adopted. He was in Paris at the invitation of French trade unionists when the state of siege was declared in December 1981. He helped to edit Polish-language Inprekor, a journal of the Fourth International circulated clandestinely in Poland from 1981 to 1990, and published "Rendez-nous nos usines!" ("Give us Back our Factories!)" (La Brèche, Paris 1985). He is at present editor of the trade union weekly Nowy Tygodnik Popularny and of the theoretical journal Rewolucja, and a contributor to internationalviewpoint.org.

[2] In the preface to The History of the Russian Revolution.

Ivan couldn't defeat Fidel

Three days of anxiety. An entire country in activity ... and without a prayer. The invincible Ivan had destroyed the fragile islands of the Caribbean. These islands are forgotten unless an event of nature is reported by the managed news media of the West. Ivan, history reminds us of the sordid stories of Czarist Russia. Storms with 250 km per hour winds, with a perfect and "a well balanced" structure, that make our specialists shudder. Ivan was born in the eastern Caribbean, touched Venezuela, hit Granada, Jamaica and any piece of land on its way. The island of Cuba stretches across the Caribbean with its thin and tranquil form. She must be asked permission to cross into the Gulf of Mexico. Geographically she is the queen of the Caribbean ... somewhat like the stories of Salgari who made us cry in our adolescence.

This Friday it was approaching Cuba from the south, "bucking" like a bronco with a rider on it. Our scientists have an impressive skill. They have to prepare models and must convince a public that is acquiring the skill day by day.

In my neighborhood there was great commotion and proposals to go to someone's house, advice on what food to prepare to withstand a lack of electricity, gas and water. Trees are cut, windows protected and Dr. Rubiera was today's Robert Redford. There was no meteorological report that the public did not hear, absolutely the entire populace. Telephone calls, messages, clues to go to the shops. By Saturday the city of Havana was a beehive. The neighbors cut tree boughs, boarded up windows, placed on safe high ground kitchen appliances.

Six o'clock in the afternoon and for three consecutive days a president forgot all official responsibility, followed with his people the rumors of Ivan. We felt that Fidel was at home. Fidel gives that impression: he makes us feel at home when we begin to lose heart.

My little son is not very interested in what Dr. Rubiera has to say. On going to bed he says in that soft little voice that gives wings to the angels, he says: "Mama, Is Ivan coming? And if he comes, do I stay home to play and I don't have to go to school? ... Anxiety clouded my eyes overflowing with tears at so much innocence confronting a monster. "No, son. You'll see, you'll see that everything will be all right. I looked around the house that had so much glass; I looked at the kitchen in which I would not warm his milk in the mornings for lack of gas. I was overcome with tears and desperation. I listen to a voice on TV ... that voice that dries tears and opens hearts. Fidel dressed in his olive green calmly expressing interest over every detail of Ivan. And the winds and the radius of the rains and what direction is it following, and if the radar of San Juan is enough, and if more resources aren't necessary to follow hurricanes, what could help our nature threatened islands ...As if it weren't enough, the oblivion to which human nature condemns us.

Dr. Rubiera satisfied him calmly and patiently. Fidel wanted to know everything and for six hours led us down the road to security ... It was as if Fidel were "the man of the house" who sealed my windows.

I asked myself: "Why does Fidel worry so much about the seasonal hurricanes? If we survive this one it would be a miracle and he is concerned about the future. This warrior who has overcome thousands and thousands of times continues to campaign. "That the two thousand and more little schools that have solar panels shouldn't have an electricity problem, that they made safe during the storm. That we must improve the radars, how much do they cost and more, if we must take into consideration the hurricanes for the plans of the battle of ideas, etc. I overcame my desperation, confidently sealing the windows.

Fidel spoke of Cuba as if talking of a barrio. His proverbial knowledge of statistics reached unheard of heights this Saturday. The colleagues of the government and Dr. Rubiera were submitted to a constant test. "We must carefully watch that zigzagging movement that does from north southwest to southwest. We cannot be over-confident".

I don't know who signs official papers these days, who would receive ambassadors or who would take care of the internal details of my country. Fidel is in vibration with his people. I felt that Fidel guided me and gave me confidence and prepared me for what was coming.

I know that many, including those of good faith, think that these are not his functions as the President of the Council of State and Ministers, that for this we have a very efficient army for civil defense and the Institute of Meteorology. But in Cuba there is a rare miracle of resonance with Fidel. Everything is tuned in; the radio and television wavelengths, the entire people and Fidel, who is not willing to fail to participate in the vicissitudes of his people by the mere fact that some European, centuries ago, had invented the Three Powers or because the world is chock full of insensitive presidents that glue themselves to papers, votes and servility.

On Saturday then, Ivan was moving along the island of Grand Cayman and its trajectory dangerously threatened us. But Fidel took us along a path of committed security, with his smile and his many expressions.

I don't know if there is a president in the world who cancels his functions to stay with his people, or if a television station stops transmitting infamous commercials and changes the programme to make this a means of connecting the people confronting a natural disaster.

And Ivan was approaching the south, threateningly with its beautiful white spiral, threatening the fragility of my coasts. If this hurricane hit Cuba we would definitely be devastated. One thing I never understood is how there could be talk of recovery. And that the supply of water, food and fuel were safe and that the chickens were protected and that the roof tile factory was making more ... For a foreign observer this seemed to be completely crazy. But in Cuba and with Fidel "this lunacy" is the greatest sensation. All expectant and sure with the chuckles of the Comandante based on that hope that Ivan would not destroy our efforts.

Sunday, Ivan decided not to hit Cuban lands. It would take to the Yucatan Strait. Of course, the westernmost point of the island would feel the hurricane winds. Almost all hurricanes hit Pinar del Rio. Fidel made them the "Owners of the hurricanes."

A blessed anticyclone in the north behaved bravely and I think we should give a name to that anticyclone. What comes to mind, for example is ... Vladimir? Through that region of the country, to the most dangerous region, personally checking all the safety measure, we had another anticyclone: Fidel... who, for 45 years, we have had the fortune of living with his skill and courage.

The eye of Ivan looked carefully and decided that this was not the right moment to confront the old gladiator, Fidel Castro, who is not even afraid of the winds and rain and like lilies here there is a rare group of persons who know how to rise up. For the Cubans, standing up is a trade. A trade against hate and arrogance. And they talk of democracy! I don't know, but I don't think there is a greater democracy where a president sits to talk directly with his people over the television. Without fearing to say something foolish, fearless of being seen with gray hairs or wrinkles or that his mike falls. He has to be with us in every hard moment.

There Ivan will go, near the United States to unleash its fury because the island of Cuba is untouchable. Because it is the island of the world.

And then they deny the permanent revolution! Those who have seen Fidel talking of the plans for emergent teachers or computer clubs or the vicissitudes of a hurricane will be seeing the authentic permanence of an unending revolution.

Now, today is a calm Monday with a slight drizzle, melancholically thinking that Fidel is not enough to make all the misfortunes of the world more bearable and that solidarity is the only alternative ... But I have just heard that Comandante Chavez has donated a million dollars to the small Grenada that was hit by Ivan.

Yes, it is possible that this new style of government is contagious and my continent will gradually be governed with commitment, love and truth.

September, 2004.

Marginal Notes on the Crime

August 20 marked another year of the atrocious assassination of Leon Trotsky. I still don't know if anyone bothered to place a flower to the flag of the Hammer and Sickle that stands guard over his remains. It doesn't matter; perhaps we aren't prepared to bury him yet. Perhaps we revolutionaries don't understand who Ramon Mercader murdered in Coyoacan.

To those who repeat to me: "you want to revive Trotsky", I answer over and over again, and each time more strongly: They will have to assassinate him again, and this time look for better and more sophisticated instruments.

And it's like this. This August 20, 64 years after his death, old Leon is more alive than ever. And, not because more people remember him but because more people need to remember him. Life is a whim of necessity and the wind is blowing to the left.

A few days ago America began to awaken. We were the Sleeping Beauty and we've have enough kisses to open our eyes. Let this mestizo maiden sleep no more!

Caracas rises up as the capital of the world left movement and surely every banner, every color, every image that recalls past times are now the same flag. There is the French July, the Russian November, the Cuban January. Internationalist Spain and the 30s, the carnations of Portugal, Allende ... still in La Moneda and much more are present. Together those who can be together. The time of reform and coexistence with the bourgeoisie has reached its end.

Sometimes in the midst of so much battling there has been an undercurrent of the struggle for economic independence, the fight against corruptions and the struggle for social justice...

And this is not a coincidence. After confusing us so much with false glimmers of globalization, neo-liberalism and extinct socialist fossils, the truth rises up like a rainbow after a heavy rain.

I am sure that the fall of the Berlin wall was fortunate. It is a shame it didn't happen sooner. The marvelous Eduardo Galeano once said, something like this: "He is not our dead...why cry over him?" He has left open the road for revolutionary action, without interference from Moscow as the master of the world left movement. The commitment is now only with our peoples and our ethics.

A German scholar said on March 17, 1883, while paying his last respects to his best friend: "The simple fact, but hidden until now in the ideological underbrush, is that man first needs to eat, drink, have a roof over his head, clothe himself before caring about politics, art, religion, etc. Therefore, the production of the immediate, material means of life and, as a result, the corresponding economic phase of development of a people or an epoch is the foundation upon which rests the development of political institutions, legal concepts, art concepts (...) and which should accordingly be explained, not the opposite that has been the case up to now."

We have forgotten and tried to do it backwards. That is so essential, like the law of the impossibility of perpetual movement. Marx made a discovery ... he did not invent anything. It is only possible to fight in depth for any political, territorial, racial and even moral demands and as a last resort, through class struggle. And I stress as a last resort.

There are times when there is no middle of the road. Everything has been tried. And, we have lost too much time and money waiting for the Earth to decide to turn in the other direction. Can you see what we have reached! The legendary Athens has many lights and soldiers. Who will tell our Greek ancestors that not even every four years do we stop taking up arms! With what increasingly puerile excuses and with such fierce destruction are they wiping out the Middle East, as legendary as the Hellenic city? More soldiers than athletes compete in the Olympics. Doping, mercantilism, changed flags and many planes and weapons to guard someone who prepares to score a clean goal or create a real record. Ah .... These conservatives, in the words of the prophet Carl Sagan , "they know not what they are conserving!".

But if we follow the road of Karl Marx ... Merely to vary ... is an implacable road. The bourgeois society is corrupt per se. Regardless how honest we are or want to be, we will become thieves if we cannot look back beyond ourselves. We steal something that is called capital gain. And this theft and another and another squashes this monster we call imperialism. There is no escape. The heritage we leave our children is pregnant with lies, sweat and blood silently supplied by the greater part of humanity, that humanity that is on the other side and is called the proletariat. It has nothing to lose and it does have a world to conquer, as declared by the Communist Manifesto. It is the only social class that has the strength to build a new society in its hands and heart. To this class only belongs the Kingdom of this Earth. And it is always the same. Regardless of any definition, the proletariat continues to be, in principle, that social class that increases the profits of the exploiters of all time. This discovery changed the path of this world. This discovery, for once, supplied us with the true weapon and has made it our only battle cry.

The worker in London is exploited just as is the worker in Northern Ireland. It's true that the Catholic workers in Northern Ireland are more exploited but always the London workers may work for those in Northern Ireland regardless of how difficult it is for us to understand. Israeli workers must be made to commit themselves to the suffering of the Palestinian people; they would be their best allies. In the same manner workers in Pakistan are exploited where the human being has learned to be as fragile as a rose and as sharp as their thorns. In the Basque country, for example, and in Catalonia they rob the proletariat with the same guile. The workers of Madrid could be the standard-bearers of this battle. It is not so complicated.

And China? A comrade explained that Karl Marx has also been forgotten in China. Is China socialist because the party says so? What party? In whose name does this party speak? Is there a socialist revolution in China? That comrade has made me stop to think. I don't know the answers. But there are workers in China. And these workers are tied to all the workers.

I count on the workers of the beautiful US people to save my revolution; to put an end to the blockade, to eliminate the lies about us. This people that organized a weekend with *Fahrenheit 9/11* would be one of the protagonists in the preservation of the Cuban revolution.

And the United States must count on the Cuban revolution to hold the joyful and internationalist country they are trying to liquidate.

And so on everywhere. These are merely some examples.

If this weren't so there would be no way to unite the proletariat and the concluding phrase of the manifesto would be erased.

I'm not unaware of the characteristics of each locality that focuses on the struggle in different forms, that the enemy vents its anger more on the poorer regions of the planet; that in our concrete actions we must consider these differences. But that is it: take them into consideration and don't make them barriers.

I am very aware that there are specific injustices against which we must be the first to offer our lives. El Che told his children, before embarking on the dream of a Latin American revolution: "Above all be capable of feeling deep down any injustice committed against anyone and any part of the world. This is the most beautiful quality of a revolutionary." Yes. To believe in the struggle for world revolution does not exclude the support of the struggle against all local and particular injustices, quite the contrary. We communists must learn to rise from the academic trenches and read more in the book of history and events. And throw ourselves into the fray as the fundamental part of the people. Our programs and books will become puffs of smoke if we don't understand this. Let's look at a case that is an example:

Julio Antonio Mella was, undoubtedly the most important revolutionary and political agitator in the Caribbean during the 20s. He founded the University Student Federation, the Anticlerical League, the Anti-Imperialist League, and the Jose Marti Popular University. But he was also, and precisely for that reason, the founder of the first Cuban Communist Party; to do so he did not have to ignore a single idea of Jose Marti, only take it to its ultimate consequences. In that first Communist Party, Marti was, undoubtedly, a member of honor.

According to Fidel, Mella "was the Cuban who did more in less time".

Mella was the most genuine revolutionary because he mentally and emotionally understood the ideas of socialism. He became the most convincing communist in the Caribbean by being the most consistent revolutionary and most committed social fighter.

The dictator Machado knew no more dangerous enemy. Neither did the Stalinist CP.

In effect, Machado ordered his death in Mexico. Mella did not have to give up being the best Cuban to be the best communist. Quite the contrary! He was the best communist by being the best Cuban patriot.

There is an important difference between being patriotic and chauvinistic. The patriot places his country within the context of international conflicts; the chauvinist is a "vain country bumpkin" who believes that the world ends within his country's borders.

Julio Antonio Mella, symbol of Cuban communist youth, was the first student of Jose Marti. More must be said about Mella.

He made the following statement precisely defending the thoughts of Jose Marti:

"The American revolutionaries who wish to overthrow the tyrannies of their respective countries cannot ignore this truth; those who claim to be unaware of its existence it is because their ignorance or bad faith prevents them from seeing the clear reality. One cannot live with the principles of 1789; in spite of the retarded minds of some, humanity has progressed and making the revolutions in this century must count on a new factor; socialist ideas in general that with one or other nuance have taken root in all the corners of the globe."

This globe is on the verge of suicide in the midst of such confusion. Chock full of cars, plastic bags, wars, terrorism and, above all, so much stupidity.

What is worse: war or terrorists? The axis of evil or the axis of good? Do we even have an axis?

This old German explained it simply but we have lost the habit of reasoning, cloaked by such cheap ideas broadcast on cable television; so much toilet paper, hunger, corruption and despair.

Without knowing about Karl Marx it is possible to reach the same conclusions. "A piece of bread and glass of water never deceives", Jose Marti said before knowing about Marx. And what about us, who is deceiving us? Imperialism in the first place. Stalinism in the second place, that which resorted to assassination on August 20, that which is even reflected in the communist organizations and subtly, imperceptibly, sprinkles us.

The right has been speechless in this battle. In its hands humanity is on the verge of disappearing. And the left? Who is the left? What is its choice? Who killed Trotsky? Did the enemy kill him? Where do we place Stalin: to the right or to the left?

August 20 gives us some clues. Let us go to the crime scene and observe the deceit in which we have lived for more than seven decades. Why didn't the so-called socialist countries ever refer to August 20? Why did Stalinism and its way of acting take over everything? It is a status quo, it has not disappeared. It is a virus that follows us with subtlety.

Engels said in a speech in front of the tomb of Karl Marx that Marx "was the most hated and vilified man of his time". True. Leon Trotsky has been even more. He was vilified by imperialism and by millions and millions of communists that were lured, unknowingly, by the sweet songs of Stalinism. That is why the victim of Stalinism was not only the inhabitant of the house in Mexico. There was another attempted assassination in Coyoacan. With Trotsky they tried to assassinate the idea of the Revolution. They managed to confuse us to some degree.

But, luckily, ideas cannot be killed. The assassination of Leon Trotsky was an attempt to kill the word within the socialist revolution. And the word is the most powerful weapon we have.

I continue to say that the truth in history is as elementary as in nature.

Although you may not know Newton's *Principia*, don't throw the wine glass because the force of gravity will take care of it; in the same manner if you do not know about Stalin's political crimes don't try to establish socialism in only one country because, like the wine glass, it will shatter the hope of whole generations. Che did not believe in Stalin although he may have said so once. He embarked on the conquest of the happiness of my continent for reasons that have as much to do with this August 20 as with any other thing, whether Che knew it or not.

Stalinism, more than Stalin himself, a mouthful in itself, has confused us. They killed Trotsky and history practically ignored him. The USSR and European socialism had to collapse to make us raise our eyes and realize that the wine glass had fallen and stained the rug and now it is difficult to remove the stain ... One of these stains fell in Mexico 64 years ago, on the head of the best Leninist. Stalinism made us believe that it was in the name of the revolution. But the only revolution that is possible was precisely the one it tried to assassinate. As bizarre as it may seem it confiscated the ideas of Marx and fell in its own trap. It was not necessary to kill so many people, so many words, such good intentions. It lies there without a USSR and without socialism. At least in Mexico the red flag protects our efforts.

Like the many headed dragon, the Revolution. It reappears every time we try to kill one of the heads.

"Alone at last", after being lost for seven decades without thinking of the importance of that August 20. No! And not another word about how good Stalinism was in the Second World War. Stalin handed fascism to us on a silver platter. That the USSR helped the young Cuban revolution? No! My revolution has lasted despite the Soviet Union.

Fidel told us once when we were hungry and uncertain, when the USSR fell (using the words of the Comandante):

"They want to give us Lenin? Fine, then he is ours." There was a nameless Noah's Ark with the purest ideas of socialism. And Trotsky is in those ideas. Who saved my revolution (I say my revolution), who made the Bolivarian revolution triumph in Venezuela but the ideas of a permanent revolution. In no way am I criticizing the revolution that Chavez is promoting. He continues in the victory with those purposes that let us win on August 15. It is not necessary that Chavez or his people define their revolution as socialist. That is not important. Nor that he take this or another measure to comply with the requests of a few sectarians. What I do know is that he intends to lift up, absolutely and courageously, his constitution and even the Gospel of the poor. He will have to face, even if he does not know it, a class struggle. And if that revolution is real, as I think it is, he will continue with his conviction of the importance of the revolution in Latin America and from there in the world.

Without a class commitment Bolivar will again have to "plough in the sea." Chavez must hold up Bolivar's wine glass. If this does not occur we will all have to plough in the sea. And there will be no wine, no revolution. Chavez, if his God helps him, must continue to look beyond his borders. The borders of Venezuela are the borders of my slender island and do not stop until the Far East. For the revolutionaries there are no borders. They are merely necessary for the Olympics.

Today, after so much manipulation there is only one way of being a true Christian, of being a true patriot, only one way of fighting for equality: Being a revolutionary. That is why they killed Trotsky: for being a revolutionary.

Let the young people be aware! We must take up a virile position before history. Let us not submit our children to have to study in Harvard or La Sorbonne to ask them later not to think. To think, doubt, question are the principal banners of the youth who are really committed to the future.

It was believed that Stalin had decided the history of the USSR. Who was left in that country but the Mafia, corruption and disillusionment? It was believed that the USSR helped Cuba in its struggle against imperialism? No way! The Cuban revolution was saved by the Cuban people and the internationalist principles of Marti, Che and Fidel. Then, what did the USSR save? It tried to save socialism within our own border. It could not. It was unable to save socialism within its own borders, simply because it is impossible. Socialism in only one country is impossible as it is impossible to halt the whim of the expansion of the universe.

A better world is not only possible, but an urgency if we do not intend to return to barbarism ... Whether you want it or not, the socialist revolution with all the ribbons and bows is the only alternative at the moment. And also it is the most beautiful and captivating of all the alternatives.

And enough of telling me that socialism is in tatters. Socialism has not triumphed yet. Socialist revolutions have triumphed. Not that many. I'm proud of having grown up in one of them. Socialism is the future, good news; it has still not come to pass.

Then let us give a vote of confidence to the Head of the Red Army. Let us give him the right to speak.

Of what he said, I only propose two principles: internationalism and permanent revolution.

These two concepts are as indispensable for socialism as hydrogen is for the water molecule. The universe had its big bang 15 billion years ago. The Moon goes around the planet, a prisoner of gravity; if we stop being childish, perhaps our grandchildren will be able to see an elephant or a whale, a product of natural selection. Genetics and cloning are a truth beyond our weeping wills. In the same manner internationalism and a permanent revolution are the necessary conditions for socialism. The struggle for socialism is the only alternative for humanity if it really plans to survive.

Comrades all: hanging over our peoples is fascism, poverty and injustice and what we are given in exchange is drowsiness and the patching up of our wounds. Let us not allow it.

By nature youth loves the revolution. All young people have the seed of change and altruism in their soul. But no young person can be called upon with half truths, with lies, with useless sectarianism and chauvinism. That is the way to build any society except the socialist one.

What was unleashed in the USSR after Lenin was anything but socialism. Socialism is synonymous with intelligence, will, action, quick responses and never servile discipline. Rosa Luxemburg said: "Socialism is precisely not a problem of knife and fork but a movement of culture, a great and powerful concept of the world."

The young are socialists by birth! We become reactionaries through our own doubts.

There, in front of our very noses is the South American revolution … One thing is clear: it's not going to wait for us. Jose Marti said: "We have to get the putrefaction out of our veins. Bad blood has to be let and the veins should be opened, swollen veins must be cut open or they drown. Either the current of the Revolution is opened or the undirected revolution flounders."

Let us toast to the current of the revolution.

It is not enough to know the truth. In the same speech by Engels that I mentioned above, he points out that: "Marx was, above all, a revolutionary." Che said the same thing: "First you must no longer exist to no longer be a revolutionary." To commit the young people to the world revolution is the first task of all communists. Without that youth there is nothing left to do. With them we will definitely take the heavens by assault.

August 20 is the day to take up the sword. Stalin is good and dead in a part of the world he intended to dominate. Let's throw Stalinism to the same place.

Trotsky, however, is fighting together with Marx, Lenin, Che…All we have to do is unite and integrate our differences into one common project.

Mella said it calling out two slogans: "…reaffirming ourselves in two principles: 'Proletarians of the world unite' and 'Together is the word of the world'. Reaffirming ourselves, not theoretically, but in practice, applying the idea to the situation."

The second phrase is by José Martí.

"The communists have but one homeland and that is the world." Mella also said it and we also have the strength of the truth behind us and the most beautiful weapons to teach it.

August 20 should be a day of combat. Using the words of the vital Silvio Rodríguez I could say that the thought they tried to erase in Mexico on a day such as this "is a book saved from the sea" and Trotsky "is a dead person who has learned to kiss."

Trotsky is reborn. We only have to sharpen the pencil point, dust off the rifle and embrace a true commitment of love.

Proletarians of the world, unite!

August, 2004.

On August 15 we take the Winter Palace

Nothing happening today can compare to what may occur in Venezuela this month. The world that is falling around us seems determined to recover, in a few days, the lost years in a collective amnesia. History openly winks at us to prevent us from letting the moment pass once again.

The brutal strengthening of the blockade of my country, using the constitution of the United States, the insecurity in Iraq, with its photographs, even overshadowing Dante and his demons; Sharon, his walls and Satanic arrogance; Kosovo ... Everything is turning Humanity into its own accomplice. The ethical decadence of imperialism is not giving that country time enough to recover the pillars of the first blessed republic of Lincoln. The Statue of Liberty will soon take on the colors of illegal French immigration.

But, I think it was Martí who said "that when there aren't many decent men there are others that have the decency of many men. These men represent thousands of men, whole peoples, and human dignity". Today, President Chavez does not have to defend the people of legendary corruption alone but he has had the chance to save human dignity that was floundering. Chavez and Venezuela must wash out the image of lies, atrocities and degradation imposed on the Earth by the darkest and most sinister frauds of the Planet, euphemistically called the "White House".

Pitched against this, the social movements are becoming more radical and politicized in weeks. What will occur this August 15 will mark the era for the left of the XXI century, this left that is gradually awakening from the silence of cheap European socialism and the evanescent cheers of neo-liberalism. Soon it will achieve its first attempt at unity. We are now aware that "La Era vuelve a parir un Corazón" [The era is giving birth to a Heart] as our Silvio entitled one of his songs.

"The time has come for our Spanish America to achieve its second and true independence", Martí pointed out. In two short months,

Venezuela is leaving the past two centuries of naive submission. And, all of a sudden our Fathers come out to give advice and share experiences.

Chavez names them all as comrades in the fight. That's what they are there for. That is the only way to keep them alive: To make their example useful.

Stupid imperialists! I repeat tirelessly "May God blind those willing to lose". Win or lose, Venezuela is carrying out a true social and political revolution on the 15th marked in a simple electoral campaign. From a strict political point of view, they have awakened a Comandante Chavez who moves rapidly to the left of the President's position. This recall referendum will not only allow the Venezuelan people to lead the destinies of America, decidedly reaffirming their intentions, but also gives Chavez the possibility of organizing an urgent revolution while in power.

One of the indispensable intellectuals of my Homeland has said more than once "the roads of America carry the civic constancy of President Allende and the revolutionary mark of Che Guevara", All right then; Comandante Chavez is at the crossroads of these beautiful tendencies.

Let's stop here for a moment:

Chavez has a marvelous quantum duality. On the one hand he has been the president of this blessed world that has been the cleanest in classical electoral terms. Seven times he has placed himself on the ballots with an almost exaggerated civic mindedness. Many comrades, including myself, are horrified when Chavez submits to a recall ballot. "Of course it was a fraud! Why does he do it?..." Of course he had to offer himself. It was a sure offer that, even with imperialism against him, he proved he could win at the ballots. It was the civic constancy of Salvador Allende pulling on his conscience.

There stands the President who swore loyalty to the Republic complete with his tricolor presidential sash. "Isn't that enough?" So now the Comandante wearing a red beret appears, reviving the sacred memories of Che Guevara. Ah, America! We have guards on every corner. It is the president who continues to be the Comandante.

On August 15, La Higuera will be victorious ... and La Moneda, all at once and always planted in the heart of only one man.

With this victory, like that of April 2002, this Homeland starts to form from the Rio Grande to the golden Patagonia and so my children will learn the significance of the incomparable happiness of a world without borders.

Of course, as observed by many comrades in the scenario of combat, it is the organized population who can best defend the President in his battle. Civilian organizations take longer to discover the directions of change. The electoral patrols and Popular Squads made up of workers and the people in general are the real shields of Comandante Chavez to win in Santa Inés. It's obvious: Chavez has given power to the people, men of dignity, for whom the Revolution was made. In these two months, almost without realizing it, Chavez is passing all power to the soviets. The social and political movements of Venezuela mature by the day. They are receiving the best lesson: these months will become a fertile period of revolutionary profundity.

I received a very serious diagnosis from Venezuela, from my colleague Sanabria, dated June 24 (El Militante). Aside from some differences of interpretation of the events, this study is an indispensable source of information and is a minute and unprejudiced observation of these actions. In the article he points out:

"One difference with the current situation is that the electoral patrols, UBEs and squads that are now rising up - and organizing hundreds and thousands, perhaps millions already, of persons - have not yet completed their work, but are barely beginning. Perhaps a sectarian dogmatic could think that today's movement is less important because it comes at the time of an electoral dispute and is born as a defensive action. If someone believes this it only demonstrates a great shortsightedness and limited knowledge of class struggle."

Exactly.

An impressive class struggle is unfolding in Venezuela without having to mention the word socialism.

Here I can make an aside: I don't like to say or hear that a country is "socialist". I mentioned this in my work "Socialism in only one country and the Cuban revolution". Socialism in only one country proved to be a complete theoretical failure. "Socialism" did not only break up in the USSR ... the "country" broke up. Not even the word socialism was left in the phrase ... or the name of the country. What does exist and remain are socialist revolutions.

Consequently comrades, don't ask Chavez to build socialism in Venezuela in the name of I don't know how many disfigured mummies. Let us save time and effort and set our sights for another second on the permanent revolution. Not only for the inhabitant of Coayacán. Before him, Bolivar did not only think of Venezuela. He could not think of Venezuela without looking over the rest of the humid and fiery land that was the object of his love and his audacity. He thought of Ecuador, thought of Peru. America was the Homeland. He only stopped to "oil the rifles".

And Martí? Paradigm of patriotism. But understood as the necessary bridge for the world.

The Cuban Revolutionary Party, undoubtedly a new kind of party made up by an exiled working class, in the majority, searching for the freedom of the islands of Cuba and Puerto Rico. Martí died trying to defend a "balance in the world" through our independence. It is mysterious and revealing. In America borders are ignored by our national heroes. In Europe they are set and braced. Even so, they moved to a single currency and speak in many languages. We could say that, in America, the desire for freedom was thought of even before other parts of the world. Permanent. Another detail: The dramatized poem, Abdala, by José Martí.

It goes as follows:
The mother love of Motherland
Is not a ridiculous love for land
Nor for the grass our feet crush
It is the invincible hatred for those who oppress her
It is the eternal rancor for those who attack her

I place this verse in block letters. The concept of Homeland for Martí is only related to a social and political purpose. The Homeland is a live commitment against its enemies. Anything else is ridiculous.

It is not passive contemplation and adoration. It is combat and action... Well, why waste more words ... "Homeland is Humanity".

Chavez looks on through the eyes of the American Homeland, to start: He was much criticized for his noble position over Bolivia and the sea. If Chavez draws on the Liberator, how to remain impassive over the demands of a people who are named after Bolivar? They don't understand us because they have gone through history stealing borders and lifting walls. Let these lands be! America will surprise us.

Then, as I see it, what Chavez can do in a revolutionary Venezuela is follow the course of Bolivar. Of course, in this century. A revolution pregnant with Projects and Missions for the people will triumph in Venezuela. A Revolution! This time Bolivar will plough fertile land and in all of South America and here lie the many Vietnams called for by that great man who hated borders.

It is perhaps the right time to beat the drums of Revolution in Latin America and jump over the hurdles. Chavez belongs to America. At times I think that many colleagues want Chavez to show his socialist passport, taking certain measures.

It is absurd! This passport is shown another way. Imperialism corners itself all alone. Chavez will triumph in the most radical process that we can imagine ... but for America, for the oil export countries, for the world. Or are we going to fall again into the trap of Socialism in only one country? Of course, anything can happen. Cuba is not Venezuela and for 45 years Bush battled with math and sought ways to get out of military service. I don't know if at that time he began to misunderstand the Bible. These are new times; there are more of us in the cart. I doubt they can blockade Venezuela. It would be funny to see New York with blackouts. Perhaps it would be a contribution towards waking up the working class of the United States.

Chavez can become an Ernesto Guevara in power.

And the socialist revolutions, amen to the indispensable role of men who have an objective expression. I don't know, it isn't even important, if Chavez has a Marxist philosophy. The ideas of the old bearded man are objective. They stand beyond our hotheads. I'll give you a simple example: Although you may not know the law of universal gravity of Isaac Newton, don't let the glass cup fall because you will undoubtedly lose it.

In social practice it is the same.

That is why I think that any transformation in Venezuela should only come from Chavez. I don't like to flatter personalities but, I think that in this case, a few comments are necessary:

In America many attractions should be found in one person to push forward a task of popular character. It is not a cult of personality but that we have the battles for our independence deep rooted. That is not what happened in Europe. The military leader, the romantic poet and personal charisma are a subconscious part of our acceptance of our leaders. The technocrats, no matter if they are honest and wise, don't attract us. If you want I can give the most recent example at hand in my country ... Chavez was imprisoned for dreaming of another Venezuela, because of his race, his religion, his patriotism framed, certainly, in an exemplary internationalism (America, the Group of the 77, etc.), it is a mirror of the best men of this part of the world and a constant evocation of our recent past of glory. Any social change in my lands should be accompanied by the dream of an American Homeland and national sovereignty. A revolution in these lands is not done without these sustaining forces.

To aspire for a radical revolution in Venezuela, even a socialist revolution will only be possible with the thoughts and popular spirit of its President or, simply, it cannot be done. I remember that something similar happened in the Chile of Allende. We must hurry to understand the social historical context of this part of the world or we will fall into the same mistakes of the past.

Sometimes I fear, in the face of so much rhetoric suffered and not understood, that many communist comrades are unaware of the responsibilities we face. The only option of all socialist parties, including those of Venezuela is to wholeheartedly back Chavez. Let's not let the same happen again! That the ghost of the communist manifesto should come out shining this time and banish from memory the ghosts of Stalinism and his warped theories. Those, I confess ... fill me with panic.

The European socialist practice silently set the same trap for us. They got us so used to the manual that we let events pass us by waiting for a phrase from the classics that would stimulate us to action. I think that something like this happened in my beloved Buenos Aires ... one December...

The Venezuelan people hold the reins now in the race of progressive ideas. Whatever happens in Venezuela will give strength to the ideas of Socialism. And, not because Chavez is one but because there, in those ballot boxes, they will be counting Karl Marx among others. Because imperialism is forced to radicalize this process with its continued stupidities. Because, already, that country "has nothing to lose" – "only its chains", to quote Marx and Engels - "they have the world to win" and we know which one.

I'll list a few curious details that illustrate the mixture of Homeland and Revolution in my lands.

Fidel Castro was not a member of the Popular Socialist Party (the communist party). He did not say that his programme was socialist. He was, however the most communist of them all, of absolutely all the revolutionaries of my country. He had the ideas of Marx and Lenin so ingrained that he did not have to stop and read or quote to explain that he was promoting a socialist revolution. When this young man attacked the Moncada he had read the socialist ideas, undoubtedly, but that didn't make Fidel a socialist for reading the works of the classics. He was a socialist for understanding it was the specific course the Cuban people needed to achieve justice. An event that didn't sit well with the PSP. The socialist revolution and communist ideas are a means to achieve happiness (the best means), but not the end.

The mention made by a colleague in reference to my previous article in reference to Che confirms this suspicion that tightens my heart. To say that Che was Stalinist because he said it in a certain context is like saying that our club won the football game because a specialist chose it as favorite. Che could say what he wanted about Papa Stalin! Che chose a communist life not by reading the difficult and revised texts of Stalin. Certainly not. He was called to this life by the illiterates, the poor, the disappeared children of America that he learned of in a unique manner, mounted on a motorcycle as a young man.

In Mexico, when Fidel and Che met, I don't know if they talked much of Marxism and theory. What I do know is that at that very moment two of the most authentic communists of the Planet Earth shook hands. Also, I don't like to say that Che was a "Trotskyist" or any other "ist". What does please me to repeat is that he tried to carry out the permanent revolution and, perhaps, without studying this theory he understood its importance and was quick to invite America to become many Vietnams. I am angry then, when someone calls Monje a communist: Failing to understand the purpose of Che and the reach of his struggle is a reproof of Monje in the most elementary Marxist terms. Lenin, Che, Fidel are authentic leaders because they know how to lay bridges between theory and actual social practice.

In the same vein, I think that without Chavez there is no revolution in Venezuela if it is not an authentic radical revolution (to avoid saying socialist)... it will never be a revolution otherwise.

Let us look up. Venezuela is the legitimate Red Army. On August 15 the Winter Palace was taken.

No doubt, not a single argument, no little phrase taken from *Capital* could say the contrary. Yes. He is a mulatto, with a poetic language of the XIX century. Yes, he is a Christian. He believes profoundly in God. But he continues to be now the creature most capable of changing the destinies of the Revolution in the world. History would not forgive us now for betraying Che in the name of communism!

The flag of the hammer and cycle was exiled from Europe. In a unique and symbolic act, Diego Rivera and Don Lázaro Cárdenas received it and buried it in that little house. There on the first border of my Greater Homeland. The ideas of Marxism-Leninism traveled with it. Left behind was the USSR. Perhaps nothing more is left. The October Revolution came here, called by Venezuela...

Now we are called upon. For several years we have been invited to watch wars of conquest and anachronistic and incoherent speeches, towers that crumble, children torn to pieces, prisoners humiliated. Sparked by Coca Cola, cigarettes and flashy cars.

In August, the Internet will turn happily to the left and we will witness the taking of power by the people. Let us join our forces to this battle. Let us form international brigades to support the Red Army and its chief from our countries and our keyboards. Today, all the communists of the world should hold a Venezuelan passport. If I had the gracefulness of Cinderella and a fairy godmother came to me, that is what I would ask for, to live through this revolution where my most sacred dreams fuse into one. The possible outbreak of a true world revolution, sung in Spanish, taking up the side of the poor.

The ghost that runs over Europe has bought herself a pretty hat and is again going around the Caribbean: Let her be.

Something seems to be forgotten: If we lose?

It doesn't matter, Chavez has already won. If we lose the President ... we still have the Comandante Fidel who did not win in the Moncada. Six years later the most authentic revolution of the West triumphed. The Venezuelan people will not need the Sierra Maestra nor the Granma ... There is one difference ... Fidel did not have us.

Cuba walked alone in America. Unfortunately there seemed to be an unmovable wall. The fall of the ill-named 'socialism' finally allows us to unite, devouring borders, languages and religious dogmas disguised with words from Lenin.

Now we can see them all: Marx, Lenin, Trotsky, Che together with Bolivar and Martí, being the first to support Comandante Chavez ... Let us sit down together, united, jubilantly singing the "International" in a thousand languages. That is what I propose for our August 15.

Workers of the world unite!

August, 2004.

"Socialism in one country" and the Cuban Revolution: A contribution from Cuba

Homeland is Humanity
-- José Martí

There is a veil of mystery over the twists and turns that helped the Cuban Revolution (CR) survive after the fall of so-called European Socialism.

For the foreign observer it might seem that the socialist revolution begun in Cuba 45 years ago has no point of contact with the tragic events that led to the collapse of the Wall last century and that the Cuban revolution is socialist for other reasons, that the warmth and sparkle of the Caribbean bestowed it with other rules governing its inexplicable vitality, in spite of the economic blockade by the United States, and the sudden destruction of relations with Eastern Europe. Perhaps that it is the leadership that has guaranteed its survival. That the Cuban Revolution today can defend its "right" to consider itself victorious from a Latin American perspective and its historical traditions and from the most demanding ethical considerations. Not at all. The CR maintains itself, among other reasons, for having been loyal to this day to the most consistent principles of Marxism-Leninism.

If the end of "socialism" in Europe is the most important negative lesson to understand the battle against Stalinism and the imposition of socialism in one country, the CR, even including its errors, is the positive lesson on the same subject. To understand the survival of the CR with its socialist character is important for the international communist movement, which now faces a beautiful battle. Now that all the Stalinist pseudo-theories, such as peaceful coexistence, socialist realism, socialism in only one country, etc., have collapsed.

There is still one resource left to the Stalinist sophists: to make a paradoxical alliance with the reformists and declare, paraphrasing Fukuyama, the end of political parties and the end of models. Truly curious. They splintered the parties, immobilizing them for action, and now want to strip any authentic party of its rights, condemning it to be rhetoric from the past. It is not that parties are useless, but that European "socialist" practice made parties futile. Parties will always be a moving force in struggles for the betterment of humanity.

Even if the name is changed due to intellectual overzealousness, as long as there are groups of people who want to change the world using political and ideological means, parties will continue to exist. Somewhat like the verses of Bécquer, of the late Spanish Romantic Period of the XIX century: "There may not be poets/ but there will always be poetry." They will not stop people from associating. What is true it that it will be the end of the Stalinist parties. Let's call things by their right names.

The same is true of models. Models can be a useful tool to simplify the study of nature and society. What happened is that, as with the Stalinist parties, the model of socialism in one country could not pass the test of history.

And here we have the Cuban Revolution, despite its poverty, defending the causes of the world from a socialist perspective. And there they are, seven European countries falling into the lap of NATO in total submissiveness. If it were not tragic it would be interesting to see how imperialism and reformism, born of Stalinism, go hand in hand against a small country that, today, is burdened not only by the battle for a better world but that defends, with its very existence, the foundations of socialist theory.

My paper will be divided in two parts. First, why I think it is time to take up Trotsky again, and second, why I believe that the Cuban Revolution rejected, from its inception, the model of Socialism in one country and thus survived after initially falling into Stalinism.

I - Why Trotsky

Trotsky's postulate, at least their practical application in social movements, were confined to small groups of Trotskyists and didn't develop fully not even in the already far off 1960s when the symbolic Che and his revolutionary instincts delayed him "only the time necessary to oil the rifle." I don't think there is a more convincing practical application of permanent revolution (PR) than that carried out by this great revolutionary and hero of the youth of the XX century, who left his posts in Fidel's victorious revolution. Before this he had been in Africa.

It was clear to Che that a true revolution and true socialism was not exclusive to the borders of my country or my continent. The flag of this legend charged with romanticism and purity was interpreted from all angles. It promoted Latin Americanism and anti-imperialism. And, in fact, it is that, but as a chapter of internationalism and the PR against the bourgeois regime. It would be like saying that Lenin and Trotsky should be considered "Europeanists" for promoting the revolution in Europe. Capitalism evolved into imperialism. Latin America became a clear scenario for social struggles, even if Che hadn't said it. We should let the literature of action guide us. Nevertheless, it is worth remembering what Che said to Fidel in his farewell letter: Fight imperialism *wherever* it shows its face. Che Guevara initiated the era of permanent revolution in Latin America. (That's how I see it.) And the foundation can be found in José Martí and Simón Bolívar, for whom the homeland was all of the Americas. José Martí went much farther. But we will leave that for later.

The fall of the Berlin wall caught us off base, as we say in Cuba in baseballese. The true Leninist militants were not seriously listened to, at least not in this part of the world. Those were not out dead; we didn't have to shed a single tear unless it was tears of happiness. Everything Trotsky foresaw in The Revolution Betrayed was furthered considerably. I wish the Twin Towers had not fallen through the actions of a few incoherent fanatics and had been the emulation of the Berlin wall. And that, instead of the planes of airlines, the revolutionary thoughts of the Americas, including the United States, had downed the ideas of imperialism and colonialism. But I think we still have time.

Since Stalin's apparent victory, which he achieved by using the most sinister tricks of Goebbels of repeating a lie ad nauseam, and murder and terror as his weapons, revolutionary forces have had two enemies: imperialism and Stalinism. An accommodation to the victory, to the real need to build a socialist republic, may lead into falling into Stalinism - without even having met Stalin. Above all for those who consider the revolution as employment. Just like with love, you can't make a business out of revolutionary ideas. It would be prostitution.

Those who hold the revolution dear and carry it in their bones and heart rarely fall into Stalinism. Fidel Castro, Cuban president for more than 40 years, rarely takes off his guerrilla uniform; he has never cut a deal with the enemy and his words always resonate with internationalism. Chávez, in the midst of his political crisis, does not stop calling for the unity of Latin America and the Caribbean. They are two authentic internationalist leaders.

Then, why Trotsky?...In the first place, because it is politically necessary. Yes. The experience of the old fighter is vital to save time and effort for the new movements. No one is preaching that people should become Trotsky fanatics. But he should be studied with the same care that we devote to Gramsci or Mariategui. There is a veil of oblivion about him and I still cannot understand the reason for it. This oblivion could force us to have to rediscover what Trotsky did less than a century ago.

Of course, no one can copy blindly. It is the spirit, the essence, that we should not throw overboard. Fortunately all the teachings that this man wanted to leave us were not obliterated by Mercader's horrible weapon. I still lose sleep at night remembering that Mercader came to my country after the triumph of the Cuban Revolution.

What I do think is absurd is that my Latin American and Cuban comrades recognize the usefulness of liberation theology but not Trotsky's thinking? I'm never given a straight answer, just sweet pats on my back and a quiet "leave that dear, its over".

Those who tell me to leave "old" affairs aside are the very same who try to reinstate (with good sense and correctly) even older thinkers but who I believe are no less necessary. Bolivar, José Martí and even Christ. The only thing left for me to say is that if religion took a new direction and that Liberation Theology has its original source in the rise of Christianity; and that therefore this theology is useful and revolutionary, by the same rights we should turn to the origins of socialism. It is time for our rebirth. Trotsky will be there, at its origin, seated and expectant at Lenin's left.

It is urgent. The blackballing of this figure in revolutionary movements can only be sustained by ignorance or by Stalinist tendencies. Stalinism, I repeat, is a dangerous evil that overtakes victorious revolutionary institutions like a sore; that takes over stagnant organisms. We have no right to lose a couple of centuries more due to puerile dogmas. We need all those who said a truth to humanity and Trotsky is one of them.

It hasn't been a long time since the Communist Manifesto, and much less since the events of Stalin's treason to the proletarian cause. Events and conferences are held from all points of view. But they don't mention Lenin. We must open the doors to a frank discussion among all revolutionaries who believe that Marxism is still one of the foundations for the salvation of the world. Let us not fall into the web of Stalinism that was woven with lies, treason and ignorance. Let us be moved by the desire to raise up the world.

Fidel Castro has repeated more than once that we will not change the name of the Karl Marx Theater nor of the Vladimir Ilich Lenin School. I am convinced that many compatriots don't know how to read between the lines.

In the most difficult moments of my revolution, when the legitimate heirs of Stalin decided to erase Cuba with the stroke of a pen, when imperialism was buying suitcases to return and my people were suffering the most atrocious poverty openly plotted by imperialism ... and Stalinism, and against all forecasts, Fidel with a strong and courageous voice shouted - Socialism or Death. That day he saved the Cuban revolution. I don't know of anything else as close to the closing words of the manifesto by Marx and Engels.

II - The Cuban Revolution, paradigm of a socialist revolution

The Cuban socialist revolution that arose in the 60s is the only socialist revolution in the Western hemisphere. It not only survived the collapse of European socialism but it is still young, it keeps up a fight without quarter against American imperialism and has been the spiritual guide for many generations and peoples. Then: Cuba, a poor and blockaded country (the pretexts used by Stalin to use this model in the USSR): Has it lasted 45 years under the banner of socialism in one country? If this is so: Is this theory valid? If not, why hasn't the Cuban Revolution fallen?

We'll find the answers in the definitions.

People don't even notice: When we talk about Cuba, we talk about the Cuban Revolution, not Socialist Cuba. The USSR never accepted the term soviet revolution, except at the beginning when it was the Bolshevik Revolution, the most beautiful revolution in the world. In these usages lies the true essence of the authenticity of my revolution and of its right to continue forward. The USSR, with all its rockets, oil and economic development, stopped being a revolution, signing its own death warrant.

The cornerstones of a socialist revolution are internationalism and the social (class) struggle without quarter.

III - Internationalism in the development of the Cuban nation.

But to understand the bond that exists between the Cuban socialist revolution and internationalism we arrive at a happy paradox: A universal outlook and social justice have been cornerstones in the formation of the Cuban nation.

Contrary to a significant number of countries, Cuba based itself as a country in being a melting pot of Spanish immigrants and African Negroes who, as journalist Marta Rojas pointed out to me, when they arrived in this land they lost their individual identity (the Galicians, Basques, etc) and were only Spaniards or perhaps "Gallegos." The "blacks" brought by the slave boats were simply referred to by that term, leaving behind the tribes and geographic regions that they belonged to.

The noted Cuban writer, Alejo Carpentier, winner of the Cervantes literature prize, concluded more or less; "We Cubans were born on the boats".

In this manner, the Cuban nation, perhaps hidden by a love for the Homeland, has its roots in two other continents with the flavor offered by American lands. In our origin, to begin with and in a very short time, three continents blended. This union becomes the substrate of our identity shaped by an exceptional anti-imperialism:

From the beginning of the wars for Independence, Antonio Maceo, military leader in the liberation wars against Spain, mysteriously expressed that the only way he would be found fighting on the side of the Spaniards would be if the United States tried to take over Cuba. He knew intuitively who, in the long run, would prove to be the real enemy without having to study socio-political treatises.

Máximo Gómez, supreme military head of the second war of liberation in 1895 was not a Cuban but a Dominican. He was respected and accepted without ever having to show his passport even once.

But Cuba's internationalist character has not had a higher projection than in the figure of José Martí. Revolutionaries all over the world still owe this man careful study of his work if we really want to understand the still controversial transition from the XIX to XX centuries.

It wasn't precisely Lenin or Trotsky who said in 1895:

"Every day I am faced with giving my life for my country and my duty, to prevent in time with Cuban independence the United States from spreading itself across the Antilles thereby falling with that additional strength on our lands of the Americas."

That was José Martí. His duty went beyond the independence of the island.

Days before writing those words, he confessed:

"But now, I can serve this single heart of our republics. The free Antilles will save the independence of our America, and the already doubtful and damaged honor of North America, and may, perhaps, accelerate and set the equilibrium of the world (...)".

Addressing a Dominican friend who wanted him to speak about Santo Domingo he says:

"Of the Dominican Republic... why should I speak? Is it a different thing from Cuba? Aren't you a Cuban? And what am I, what land ties me down?"

José Martí made his ideal of internationalism the ultimate goal of Cuban independence. He had the opportunity to get to know the United

States well, and in his poetic and elevated language described nascent imperialism better than any other being (That's how I see it).

That is why the second stage of the struggle, the revolution of the 1930s where the young people, in addition to fighting the tyrant, Machado, had another front that was based on internationalist ideals: the Spanish republic. When the government of the moment did not allow a ship from the young soviet republic to dock, Julio Antonio Mella (of whom Fidel said that this was the Cuban who had done the most in the least time and was the founder of the first Communist Party) took a boat and, representing the Cuban people, reached the ship and joined in brotherhood with all the crew. This young man, incidentally, was expelled from the party he founded. At the time, it was still possible to talk of the International and it restored his membership. He died murdered in Mexico. Dying he did not mumble some jingoistic slogan but passed into immortality saying, "I die for the Revolution".

Fidel Castro's revolution also marched along the road of the world. In a letter written to Celia Sánchez in 1958, Fidel confessed:

"When this war is over another longer and greater war is ahead: the war I am going to fight against them (the Yankees). I am aware of what is going to be my true fate.

After 45 years, we are perplexed to observe that he has kept his word.

And, of course, we still have the image of Che, the classic symbol of true internationalism. Che abandoned his family, responsibility, honors to fight in other lands that "call for the help of my modest efforts".

I know a close friend of Che who commented to him the incredible acceptance of the independence fighters to accept Máximo Gómez, a Dominican, as head of the general staff. This comrade relates that Che looked at him with half a smile. Only then did the comrade realize he was talking to an Argentinean. Che did not have the same experience in Bolivia. On the other hand, I do not believe that there has been a better example of the rigorous application of the permanent revolution.

These are just a few examples.

Social Justice: the other cornerstone of the Cuban nation

Our war of independence was belated in comparison to the other American nations. This allowed, however, the leaders to mature in the experiences of European revolutions and put forth very advanced and radical principles in what was supposedly a mere war for independence. Contrary to what occurred with the Declaration of Independence of the United States in 1776, that deleted the principle of abolishing slavery, which would cost that country another war in the following century, the insurrection for the liberty of Cuba is proclaimed together with the abolition of slavery. They were two arms of the same body and neither was possible without the other. In fact, landowner Carlos Manuel de Céspedes frees his slaves and invites them to fight for liberty as equals.

When, after 10 years of war, the Spaniards manage to impose the signing of the Zanjón pact, Antonio Maceo reproaches the Spanish officer that is supposed to convince him to join the surrender even though the pact does not provide for the abolition of slavery, and that for that reason as well as others he would continue to fight. At the end of the meeting, Martinez Campos says, "Then we don't understand each other" to which Maceo responds: "No we do not".

José Martí founded the Cuban Revolutionary Party in 1892. I insist that his contribution to universal politics and philosophy are a pending subject for those of us who try to understand the course of history. The basis of this Party goes beyond the mere independence of the island. Its projection, its internal organization put it in the category of a party of a new type. Its main recruiting ground was the working class! (Tobacco workers in exile). It is founded before Lenin's Party. The differences between Europe and America will make the superficial reader see incompatible points between the two. For the careful and patient reader, absolute and common truths will be revealed mysteriously. This revolutionary Party would give birth to the Cuban Communist Party 30 years later. Carlos Baliño was a founder of both, and knew that they were one and the same thing.

It would be redundant to talk about the vocation for social justice of the revolution that Fidel Castro leads. As simply one more detail to be analyzed in greater depth is the manifesto, History Will Absolve Me. This is Fidel's defense after the attack on the Moncada Garrison. I still cannot understand how imperialism failed to see that this was an authentically communist document. The social problems are highlighted and a class profile of the Cuban people made that would leave breathless the most orthodox socialist anywhere in the world. This document was written 50 years ago and still maintains its freshness and most demanding logical order. Six years later, against all predictions, joining in its spirit social justice and internationalism, a profoundly socialist revolution triumphs under the very noses of imperialism, as someone once said.

Final notes

In Che's farewell letter to Fidel he points out that the most sacred duty was to fight imperialism where ever it may be. Imperialism is very close to us. That is why simply by existing Cuba makes its greatest contribution to the cause of universal socialism. Don't be mislead I do not think that the Cuban revolution is immortal, per se. I believe we have made serious mistakes. In fact, in 1986, Fidel calls for a "Rectification of errors and negative tendencies", against the bureaucracy and other problems, pushing society forward with more verve. This was before the cheap jargon of Gorbachov about perestroika and glasnost. You just have to see where these types ended up. It would be interesting to analyze who they were heirs to.

As dialectics teaches us through unity and the clash of opposites, the counterrevolution is an entity that grows in the shadow and is waiting for the first misstep. I doubt that any country has such a hostile exile community as ours. Our only way is to be ever more radical, more consistent with our vitality, which have been internationalism and social justice. Any attempt at congruence with imperialism (note that I separate from this the noble people of the United States, with whom we must have an ever increasing relationship) would be a step back on our road. Because the revolution has no end; we already know what an old and forgotten comrade pointed out, the revolution is permanent.

On the world stage there is a new and unprecedented revolutionary situation. The Bolivarian Revolution in Venezuela is just that: a Revolution. Chavez unceasingly talks about Latin American unity. Chavez's revolution will be safe as long as it does not compromise with the enemy and becomes ever more radical.

Trotsky also dreamed of this unity while in Mexico. It is a shame that Stalin did not let him live. No matter. His breath (although many hold deep prejudices) will be in revolutions that will arise sooner or later. We will take him up from this silence and make him be seen, without considering him a terrorist. A strange thing, that: the imperialists and the Stalinists were in agreement in calling him a terrorist. A point in our favor.

The advantage Cuba may have had is that she carries in her marrow two of the most important bastions against socialism in one country. Fidel is not a biological accident. Fidel is, just like Martí, a product of all the elements that form us as a nation. The Cuban revolution can be eternal if it continues to be a revolution; projecting itself and living for the world and for the dispossessed. It will die out without pity in its history the day it decides to stop and try to become a completed republic.

Workers of the World Unite!

Published by Tricontinental, May, 2004.

The Flag of Coyoacán

On November 7 we will be celebrating the 96th (now the 97th) Anniversary of the forgotten October Revolution, the revolution that shook the world in 1917 and scattered to the winds fears and myths; that opened to the world the doors of a new project; that gave Marxist theory firm bases. Of this glorious revolution, in spite of its resounding and apparent end it joins all who hope that a simple event will save the world. No mistake should be made: the revolution that sang out in the cruiser Aurora, and in the Winter Palace is not the one that ended in the fall of 1990 when some men, completely alien to it decided that they did not sit well with Socialism and toasting with imported vodka, crossed over to the other side. The glorious revolution of the Soviets was no more (thank God) and this wishy-washy government slid down until the eighties of the twentieth century.

But History always surprises us with its strange coincidences: On November 7, 1878, one of the most principled revolutionaries of all times was born. Lev Davidovich Bronstein, known as Leon Trotsky, admired by some and hated by others ... forgotten by the majority, except by stubborn events. At 125 years since his birth, faced with the incapacity of capitalism to offer humanity an alternative for survival and the disastrous backlash of European socialism, we stand in front of a small house in Coyacán, Mexico. The flag with the hammer and sickle, last symbol of the socialist revolution, continues to wave in silent tribute to the death of its last inhabitant.

Trotsky and Natalie do not rest in Russia ... In Russia is the Romanov family. The Czar, buried with military honors and great pomp, presided over by those who were once communist leaders. The truth of socialism in Europe does not rest in the old continent. But in mystical Mexico, the Latin American continent has awakened to the fact that social struggle is the only road towards equality.

Not finding asylum in Europe the old revolutionary was received by the brush of Diego and the sensuality of Frida and the revolutionary

Lázaro Cardenas. The destiny of Marxist principles was joined there with the most symbolic avant–garde art in this part of the world. This region that does not wait for norms, nor for methods to conquer its freedom and justice. There are the last events that speak for themselves. In each is the seal of the old German, Karl Marx. Since Marxism does have scientific bases and the truth does not wait for eyes to see it nor skill to foresee it.

After the last decade of last century when the world collapsed in the imagined end of history in the hands of neo–liberalism, the Russians hand in hand with the grandchildren of the "Stalinist terminators", began hysterically to tear down statues and carried off the body of Lenin that burned their hands like a hot potato, not knowing where to bury him. They tried to turn back the clock, reviving Princess Anastasia, etc. And they fell to the most depressing and abject system ever known. The Mafia ruled by the old Central Committee leaders held a dark power, the same kind of the bureaucratic and sinister power that did away with the left wing bases of the authentic Bolshevik party, the same power that killed the international communist movement and made it an ideological colony of Stalin, the same power that transformed the wonderful ideas of Lenin into pathetic norms, that struck out revolution from communist philosophy, canonized socialism in only one country. What the USSR did after the inopportune death of Lenin was not socialism in only one country. It was not socialism; it never was … now we see that it was not also a country. The USSR shattered into bits. Oh, those who think that history can be measured in days! … Its beat is another and the end of this model is now evident.

It is criminal then that today's left-wing movements, at times, stop talking of Marxism and Leninism, because of the resounding end of the USSR. This collapse has been the best argument to have faith in those revolutionaries who thought that internationalism was the building block of the triumph of those ideas. This end demonstrates how right Lenin and his followers were. The dark power of Stalin put an end to it all. Not even the defeat of fascism can redeem him from trying to strip intelligence, dedication and audacity of socialist ideals.

Trotsky was the last of the contemporaries of Lenin, of the leader of the working class. This dark power managed to lie, barefacedly, about the head of the Red Army, accusing him of being crazy and a terrorist and even an accomplice of Hitler. Not content with his work, Stalin used his power to have Mercader assassinate Trotsky on August 20… What he fortunately was unable to do was to remove the flag from Coyoacán. When monuments and ideas of the USSR crumbled and the world with

Fukuyama shouted incoherently, when all the revolutionaries of the world closed their eyes in horror and the reactionaries rubbed their hands with glee, in Coyoacán the flag of the hammer and sickle continued to flutter in the wind of ancestral Mexico, like a mysterious symbol.

Many comrades tell me that, although this is true, too much time has passed and ideas have taken another route, that another phase of imperialism was born in New York on September 11 with the destruction of the Twin Towers. The militarism that Petras has described so well like a new phase of imperialism needed new forms of struggle, that there is now the Internet, and that the world is unipolar ... What point is there in bringing Leon Trotsky back to life? Simple. In history, to forget is a sin. José Martí, the visionary of America, said that "he who sets aside, by will or forgetfulness, a part of the truth, in the long run will fall due to the truth he left out, which grows neglected and crushes that which rises without it".

To turn back is necessary, now that it is evident that history is beginning. It is going forward and not turning back. Che said, more or less, that if a pilot loses his way he must not turn back to the point where he got lost. He must return to port and then try again. For all those of us who think that socialism as set down by Karl Marx, enriched by many later, is the true road to peace, justice and solidarity, we will come back to that forgotten point. To avoid mentioning Marxism and its spin offs for fear or for being popular can lead us back to the dangerous crossroads. At the age of 70 Galileo Galilei recanted his heliocentric theory for fear of the Inquisition. Nonetheless the Earth continues to revolve around the Sun.

When we search for that road towards an equilibrium between man, nature, power and freedom, unknowingly we will be going along the routes of Marxism and we will stop, still without realizing the crisis of the twenties and thirties in the USSR, we will understand that these roads, even as mere references, have a stop off in Coyoacán.

Engels once said that bourgeois society confronts the quandary of moving towards socialism or turning back to a state of barbarism. In other words, socialism or the collapse of civilization. I hesitate to think of the distance that separates us from both extremes. But the sooner we are aware of this truth, not half heartedly nor with reformist rhetoric, the less we will be impelled towards the veritable end of human history ... when we disappear as a species. Then we would be in a universe without memories. I am fully aware that there are prime directives to fight for: peace; the preservation of the planet; our function as an intelligent species gifted with a conscience. Yet we must understand that the only road to peace and social justice is socialism. Peaceful coexistence and all its fallacies have tragically lost their opportunity to triumph. With the exploiting classes there will never be social justice; without social justice there will never be peace.

The communists of today must not fear being singled out from the destroyed socialist bloc. That was not socialism, that revolution was betrayed.

We must recover memory and rise from that state of collective amnesia in which we want to sheath the new movements. The Marxists have much to offer the people in the midst of desperation confronting realities that are misunderstood. Enough of falling back on the rhetoric of the enemy: "terrorism, national security". Let us lift up our old weapons. Never before has the world been more convinced that its salvation is through unity or it will disappear. We have lost too much space. Let us take up the slogan of Trotsky who, on the eve of his contemptible assassination, declared with conviction: "whatever the circumstances of my death I will die with an unyielding faith in the communist future".

Let's join the people under the banner of the International. Never before has the world needed, as now, to remember November 7. As never before must we understand that the banner of Bolshevism never died, that it was exiled in Europe and reached America to cure its wounds in silence, in irredentist Mexico. This Mexico that quietly marched that October 2 carrying the red flag of Coyoacán that it has taken up. And let us shout to our enemies, regardless of whether they call us terrorists, that we will not fight for the imperialist war, or for the miserable peace of injustices; we will fight together for the socialist revolution in permanent combat.

Workers of the World, Unite!

Published by the Haydée Santamaria Association for Peace and Solidarity, December, 2003.

Yeyé's Victory

> *Thank goodness, there are people who*
> *are willing to risk everything—even their lives. . .*
> *They die without complaint, knowing*
> *they will live on after death. . .*
> Silvio Rodríguez

Even after so many years, Mama still exerts a strong influence on my brother Abel and me. Speechlessly, we feel her heart beat in every piece of furniture that left her house, and her acute and intelligent view is what moves an antique footstool or vase from one place to another.

Nothing we have has ever belonged to us; we did not inherit anything. In some way, she ordered things this way, and that's how it's been. The love and strength with which she viewed everything protects her property.   She was skilled in more spheres than most other revolutionaries were – and she was indeed a revolutionary. I've never had a better example so close to me, but, in order to imagine her well, so that my children and yours may know her, try to combine the independence of a Madame Bovary with the purity of Joan of Arc – or, more simply, the intimate poetry of Anne Sexton and her "Wanting to Die" with the head-on, deeply-rooted, singular commitment of Fidel Castro's Revolution, in which she began to live right from the beginning, as this book [1] makes perfectly clear. That Revolution, which entered the narrow doorway of her and her brother Abel's apartment at 25th and O Streets, which she had assigned herself the task of keeping clean – a revolution which now, 50 years later, seems to be the world revolution – lay at the heart of the existence of that woman, my mother, who cherished it just as she cherished each one of us.

Time and again, she told me that she trusted Fidel completely right from the beginning and that Fidel should live for a long time, for her and for Abel. [2]   We are absolutely convinced of this now, but half a century ago, only the special light that shone in those Santamarías showed how important a man such as Fidel Castro was for the Cuban Revolution. She stated this in the letter she sent to my grandparents from the Guanajay jail for women, which is included in this edition.

With an almost childlike simplicity, she begged her mother to be happy over Abel's death and noted that they had already experienced "great and wonderful changes," which was true: my grandmother, who had put down deep roots in Spain, ended her days fighting for her Constancia Sugar Mill with impassioned fervor and serving in the ranks of the Communist Party.

Even so, the attack on the Moncada Garrison was just the beginning. Everyone who really knew her recognized that she stood up well when faced with the terrible aftermath of the action; she did not crumble, even on being shown Abel's eyes lying in a washbasin. After those horrors, Haydée was a much stronger person and did much more. Abel was the first person she had loved with her entire being, but she drew strength rather than weakness from his death. She knew that she, along with all of the other enlightened ones, was in the eye of the storm.

The attack on the Moncada – with the deaths of her fiancé, Boris [3] , and of Abel – was just the beginning for her. Thinking back now, for example, I do not know how Fidel could manage to keep her from going down to the civil hospital despite how dangerous it might have appeared. Ever since she first began ironing the fighters' uniforms, she was a part of that history, and, in the years following that tragedy, she met and grieved for other loved ones, too.

In the underground, she was in her element. She had scores of anecdotes about my father's inability to hide. She recognized that the young lawyer Armando Hart had the unique qualities and intelligence needed for Fidel's venture, such as a depth of political understanding and the ability to incorporate all honest ideas into a project. I can testify to the singular love she had for him and the respect with which she taught us to love him as more than just a father. Her priority was to guide my father's special ability to benefit the Revolution.

Concerning Frank País [4] , she told me that they needed his dedication to the cause, his seriousness and his sense of discipline. Mama gave the impression that she was building a Noah's Ark in which to protect the most virtuous and capable of the Cuban people, selecting subjects for a watercolor, making a synthesis of the purest human beings of her time and place. Then, if I naively asked her why we needed Frank, she would turn her large, mysterious eyes on me and reply in a low voice, as if she were still in the underground, "For this, Celia María, to create this." She never told me just what "this" was, but she did not need to. I know what it is now, though it took me many years to understand.

We must remember her that way, filled with light and the joy of giving herself to this never-ending, inspiring work of Fidel's.

Two figures stand out from what she told me of her time in the Sierra Maestra Mountains: Che, about whom I will comment later, and Celia [5], for whom I was named. Even when I was a little girl, she would tell me, "When people recognize you because of your last names [Hart and Santamaría], say that your first name comes first, that you are called Celia for Celia Sánchez and that it is the name you must live up to. Your name is the best present I have given you; learn to respect it." Knowing that Celia was close to Fidel gave her great peace of mind; and Celia's death, a few months before her own, moved her to incredible limits. Through her tears, above all else, what she would say was that who we should concern ourselves with was Fidel: "who would care for him like Celia?"

With the triumph of the Revolution, another stage in the struggle began. My paternal grandmother, Marina, kept telling her and my father, "It's all over; relax," but that is precisely what true revolutionaries cannot do. Those who are made of sterner stuff never know peace, for they cannot be content with what has already been accomplished, but must always keep raising their sights.

Using Fidel's purest ideas and the warmth and ability of her own spirit, that enlightened woman took on the project of building a new world, the doors to which the inspiring decade of the '60s opened with a salute. Offering the possibility of being happy, creating, inventing, flying, and giving wings to Silvio Rodríguez's [6] first lyrics or to the fresh and dancing words of Gabriel García Márquez [7], and learning – without plucking the petals of daisies – who would be her allies in that great endeavor.

Just as when Celia died, Che's death was a terrible blow. When she talked to me of Che, she suffered even more than when speaking of her brother Abel. She told me, "I can hardly imagine the Revolution without him," and "How will Fidel manage without Che's support?" But Che went on to his reward, and she continued her struggle. Every October 8, my brother Abel and I would stay inside, poring over Che's letters to his children, and, ever since – perhaps because dusk comes early in October or maybe because of that custom – I am visited with a special melancholy on October 8.

I went to high school with Che Guevara and Aleida March's second child, Camilo, and I remember that I considered him to be somebody special, because he was both dauntless and above reproach. Even so, I got mad at him every so often. Whenever this happened and I told Mama about it, she would say, "Just take care of him. Don't let anybody criticize a child of Che's." It was not hard to do this; Camilo won everybody's respect and affection without ever trading on his last name.

A weekend wouldn't go by without her telling me something to make me feel that Che was a part of me, saying that it hurt her that I had not known her best friend. She considered that lack an "original sin." Effortlessly, as if with a magic wand, she created moods and atmospheres that helped me get to know him.

Right from the very beginning, Mama felt Che Guevara's charisma, the undeniable force that his image of hope would mean for the coming generations. In observing all of the special people who dedicated themselves to Fidel's venture in one way or another – Abel, Frank, Che, Celia and many more who flocked around him, bringing out mankind's need to dream in order to build reality – her purpose was always the same: to help them to support Fidel, that giant who raised his times to new heights on the wings of love and courage. That purpose is more important than ever now, in the new millennium, which has so few myths and outstanding figures.

In the letter she sent to Che after his death – that Ocean Press published again recently – she spoke to him as if knowing he was listening.

She always insisted on our having high ethical values. I remember that Celia Sánchez gave me a wonderful box of dolls on one of my birthdays – I must have been seven at the time. After letting me enjoy the surprise for a while, Mama said, "Now choose one and give the others to your friends who don't have Celia to give them presents." That experience, which was similar to what José Martí described in "Bebé and the Distinguished Mr. Pompous," made a great impression on me, for life had picked me up and made me a character in that story, calling on me to act as unselfishly as Bebé had done. I still dream about those dolls, but I learned that you get a good feeling from giving with love. That was how she taught us.

More than an advantage, having her for a mother – especially for my brother Abel and me – implied a commitment that I could barely identify. Every year, the number of our brothers and sisters grew. My family welcomed everybody who was trying to assimilate grief. I have fond memories of Víctor Jara, his voice filled with sadness and love, and of the beautiful Milena Parra, whom I was supposed to take care of and give my most beautiful dolls to, because she was Violeta Parra's granddaughter, and, many others.

I also remember when I was very little, that somebody with a guitar came to the house. He was very sad about something. It may have been Silvio Rodríguez, Pablo Milanés or Vicente Feliú [8]. I never knew who, but I remember that lightning bolts of a bad storm were falling with sharp cracks in front of the choppy winter sea. "Some day, we'll get electricity from that dangerous lightning," Mama said. I never understood the relationship between fear and happiness, but the young man picked up his guitar and began to sing, and was happy again.

Mama hated all unnecessary formality, and that reigned in the Casa de las Américas, her "house in Vedado." There, using the weapon of love, she imposed her own way of doing things. The mockery and scorn for bureaucracy in the younger generation is summed up in a drawing that the painter Mariano Rodríguez drew on a paper napkin during a meeting of the Board. She was his boss, and the only minutes he kept of the meeting – or, at least, the only ones that have been preserved – consisted of that napkin, which hangs on one of my walls today. I can still see those meetings, filled with straight talking; I envision them as a galaxy of stars shining in bright contrast to the mud of every day.

When I was 12, she decided that I was madly in love with Roberto Fernández Retamar [9], — which I really was, by the time I turned 13. I confided my secret to Adelaida de Juan, my Quixote's wife. I still have the photo that she made him give me, and the tiny vase in which, every other day, I was to place a white rose because "Roberto has always loved Martí very deeply and tenderly and to love Martí, you must do so in the same way."

That love left me with a deep admiration for Roberto and Adelaida and a sentimental, virginal love, for José Martí, which subsequent studies of his works have only enhanced. When I read Martí, I still smell the perfume of the white rose and feel the ribbon with which Mama lovingly tied my hair before I went to bed. I am linked to Martí with the indestructible, passionate love of an adolescent – a kind of love that I have never felt for anyone else.

Mama never went beyond the sixth grade, but for them, the enlightened ones, that was enough. Her love of life exempted her from any academic requirements. That summed her up: a wanderer who was happy with what she saw. I think that my brother and I, the "genetic heirs" of her approach toward life, are in basic accord with that. The inspired words of Abel — my Abel, who doesn't speak much — make up for his prolonged silences.

We have no choice but to respect those who decide that it's better to be dead than alive. People say that animals don't commit suicide unless it's to defend their young, so suicide is a very human way to die. The old idea that revolutionaries never take their own lives (as she, too, used to tell us) is childish, as just a few names will show. The Lafargues decided that they would be more useful to the cause of the proletariat dead than alive, and I'm sure they were right.

Who dares to say that the bell, which Hemingway tolled with his pen, didn't make the bells in all the churches in the world echo to the sound of his last bullet? Who could think that Violeta Parra didn't give thanks to life with honesty before going to her death fearlessly, sure of herself, leaving us the candor of an entire continent in her voice?

Then all that is left is to bow our heads and shed tears of pity – for ourselves, not them, who are more alive than dead. Who move through the boundary between the two states of matter, freely and without pain, and keep us from making mistakes. We are irreversibly destined to die, but not them.

For those for whom only measurable things count, there is the Casa of love, which Haydée founded; there is the Americas, to which she was devoted, for she felt its tremulous, confused heartbeat when she joined herself to its heralds. Let them respect measurable things, then – those whose hearts don't beat in harmony with the hearts of others, those who don't understand these things because they can't feel them and those who think that the ones who have more wisdom in their souls are mad. My message of gratitude is for the enlightened, both living and dead, as Silvio shouts in his [song] "menos mal que existen" (better they exist).

There's one more thing. I am – or was – her daughter, and I lived on after she died, surrounded by some of the living dead in a world in which Cuba exerts a gravitational and magnetic pull as the epicentre of the people's struggles for a better world – the world as it should be, after 15 billion years of striving for harmony. She left me safe and provided for here, where I can work for good alongside Fidel whose name so many people intone with their last breaths, and wildly in love with Martí.

So, then, our final victory – Yeye's [10], too – is linked to the attainment of happiness on a certain blue planet in a solar system in the Milky Way. Perhaps, a few centuries from now, its inhabitants will say, "Our good fortune may very well be linked to a tiny apartment on a small island in our not-very-large planet. The Earth is happy; now, we should turn our sights to the sun."
2003.

NOTES

1 This text is taken from the prologue of the first biography of Haydée Santamaría's, in the process of being published by Ocean Press.

2 Abel Santamaría Cuadrado, second in command of the July 26 Movement. At only 25 years of age, he was taken prisoner on the morning of the 26 of July of 1953 along with a valiant group of compañeros. The Batista police savagely tortured him; they took out his eyes and showed them to his sister, who was also in jail, to get her to talk. They assassinated him that same day. Of him Fidel would say, "He was the soul of the Movement."

3 Reynaldo Boris Luis Santa Coloma, Haydée's fiancé during the underground struggle against the Fulgencio Batista dictatorship, integral member of the M-26 Civil Committee and among those who stormed the Moncada barracks. He was taken prisoner by the Batista assassins, horribly tortured and assassinated.

4 Frank País García, young underground fighter and prestigious revolutionary leader of the Orient zone of the island, M-26 chief of national action, assassinated on July 30 1957.

5 Celia Sánchez Manduley, along with Frank País, organized and directed the reinforcement units sent to the Sierra Maestra Mountains. Later she too joined the guerrilla struggle along with Fidel Castro in the Eastern mountain range. After the war, she created the Office of Historic Affairs and carried out other State functions until her death in 1980.

6 Singer and songwriter, member of Movimiento de la Nueva Trova Cubana.

7 A Colombian writer.

8 Members of the Movimiento de la Nueva Trova Cubana.

9 Cuban poet, essayist and director of the Casa de las Americas.

10 A familial nickname for Haydée.

Mom, jail and happiness

It's been 50 years since my mother was let out of jail at Guanajay. I have visited her cell more than three times. I still don't accept in a conscious way that that radiant and happy woman – that woman who could create a party with a pitcher of water, the one who combed my hair, that made the Casa de las Américas the wellspring of enthusiasm, she who made me adore Silvio's music when his songs were heard only from his adolescent voice – that same woman, was a prisoner along side Melba in a small dark cell. She lost her brother and her boyfriend, and the only thing she had left was her wounded and burning homeland and a man who would be the one who saved her.

It is still an enigma how Haydée could rely on the belief that Fidel was alive to follow the path, how she stood up to everything and everyone so that finally Cuba and Fidel would coincide, like a premonition, like a sacred encounter. I still tremble, when I read her letter, which follows these words. My grandmother should understand that her son Abel was not as important as Fidel and should be happy because a stranger had survived Moncada and not her son... it seemed like madness because of the pain... Some years later, my grandmother Joaquina committed herself so strongly to Cuba and to the people of the Encrucijada sugar mill that few would accept that she was Spanish. That madness of Haydée was the announcement of a great truth: my grandparents died in Cuba struggling for their people just like any other two Encrucijadans.

The picture, which is so well known, taken in Guanajay on the Day of the Three Kings in 1954, cost lives. I don't want to think, to be morbid, about the suffering of my mother while she leaned back on the little gray beds. Her mind must have flown high and I believe, or I want to believe, that after thinking of her brother – who for me is the saint of the family, because I have yet to find anyone to tell me one defect – she dreamt of Casa, about us, with so many, many good people she met later. I want to believe that as she decreed that Fidel was what Cuba needed, she must've thought that the Casa de las Américas, with its vibrant multitude, my brother Abel and me were indispensable for her. That this impulse accompanied her seven months, that book by José Ingenieros and its moral forces would announce a near future full of love and commitment beside my father, that she would be the director of an orchestra of North American angels, or that she – with only the rudiments of an education – would come to foretell who in my country, would sing, paint, or become a professional writer.

At this fifty-year distance, and more than twenty since her death, I believe I am happy thinking, that when that thin and sad girl crossed the hall door of the prison of Guanajay, that just as in a novel about knights, she knew that what awaited her was a permanent struggle alongside the best lineage of the Cuban people... An old German man with a beard and talent said that the struggle was his idea of happiness.... My mother reached the highest levels of that happiness. From what I remember, she never stopped being on a campaign.

Letter that Haydée Santamaría Sent to her Parents from the Guanajay Jail, 1953

Now I'm at Guanajay. I've been meaning to write you ever since I got here, but I knew you'd heard from Elena and Manuel that I was here and that I was OK.

I've been here for about 15 days. I thought it would be better to wait a few days before writing and telling you something about what it's like here and what you have to do to come. If you can come and if they let you bring children, bring Carín [1] with you. They might tell you that you can bring them. Visiting hours are on Sundays, from 2 to 6 p.m.

I want you to know that I'm very well, and you shouldn't worry about coming. Lots of people come every Sunday, and bring us all sorts of things. The food is good, so you shouldn't worry. Tell me ahead of time which Sunday you're coming – you aren't allowed to come more than once a month – so nobody else will come that Sunday, and I can be with you all the time and not have to spend time with other people who live nearby and can come any Sunday. So, let me know before you come. Again, I am fine. Except for your worrying about me and for knowing how sad you are, knowing that Abel will never be with you again, I could almost say I was happy. If you thought about Abel the way I do, you, too, could feel – well, not happy, but not as crushed as I know you are.

Mamá and Nino [2], I know that nothing I can tell you will take away your terrible grief. Perhaps, after some years have passed, you will understand me and be convinced that you are privileged parents who will always have your son with you. And you will have him just as he was – good, young and handsome. That son will never get old and ugly and cranky, the way the others will. Abel was, is and will always be a son who doesn't grow old. He will always have a handsome face. For you and for all of us, he will always be strong and filled with infinite tenderness. He will make us better people; he will always be our guide. And, for you, he will be your closest child. Think about it: you've already experienced changes – great and wonderful changes – which, alone, would make me accept what's happened and be almost happy. Abel has made you Cubans; Abel has made you love this land, this beautiful land where he was born and which, I think, is the only thing he loved more than you.

You may think you won't have Abel any more, but, from Santa Efigenia Cemetery [3] , he has told you to love Cuba and Fidel. He asked this of you before, but it's only now that you have understood this truth, and, even if I never saw you again, I would be proud of you because you have lived up to being Abel's parents.

Mamá and Nino – but especially you, Mamá – you used to tell me over and over again that Abel was the only one I loved, that he was the only one in the family who mattered to me, yet I'm going on living and haven't been crushed. Why, then, can't you go on living, too, and not let yourselves be crushed? You must go on living for him and love what he loved so much. You should spend your lives defending what he gave his life for: the Constancia workers [4] , not the Luzarragas [5].

Mamá, you still have Abel. Don't you see this, Mamá? Abel will always be with us. Mamá, remember that Cuba exists and that Fidel is alive to make Cuba the kind of country Abel wanted. Mamá, remember that Fidel loves you and that Abel believed that Cuba and Fidel were the same thing. Fidel really needs you. Don't let any mothers say bad things about Fidel to you; Abel wouldn't forgive you if you did.

NOTES

The original text has been subjected to a few corrections to improve its comprehension.
1 Haydée's niece who was just a baby then.
2 An affectionate nick-name Haydée used for her father Benigno Santamaría.
3 The cemetery at Santiago de Cuba.
4 The Constancia Sugar Mill, today the Abel Santamaría Cuadrado.
5 A reference to the name of the exploitative landholders of the area where the Santamaría Cuadrado family lived.